Where Two Are Gathered

Readings for Shared Devotions

April Yamasaki

BRETHREN PRESS
Elgin, Illinois

Where Two Are Gathered
Readings for Shared Devotions

BRETHREN PRESS, 1451 Dundee Avenue, Elgin, IL 60120.

Cover design by Kathy Kline Miller

Library of Congress Cataloging in Publication Data
Yamasaki, April.
Where two are gathered: readings for shared devotions/ April Yamasaki.
p. cm.
ISBN 0-87178-943-4
1. Married people—Prayer-books and devotions—English. 2. Bible. N.T. Matthew—Devotional use. I. Title. II. Title: Where 2 are gathered.
BV4596.M3Y35 1988 88-17651
242'.84—dc19 CIP

Manufactured in the United States of America

Two are better than one, because they have a good reward for their toil. For if they fall, one will lift up his fellow; but woe to him who is alone when he falls and has not another to lift him up. . . . And though a man might prevail against one who is alone, two will withstand him.

Ecclesiastes 4:9–12a

Contents

Introduction

These devotional readings are designed for two individuals to share together. This may be a husband and wife planning to read Scripture together regularly, two prayer partners needing a focus for their time with God, or two friends interested in exploring worship. Whatever the stage of personal relationship, these devotional readings seek to deepen both partners' commitment to God and to each other.

On the following pages are fifty-two devotional readings to read aloud throughout the year, as well as a set of special readings for Thanksgiving, Christmas, and Easter. Each of these readings includes a brief introduction, a responsive reading built around a passage from the gospel of Matthew, and some concluding thoughts for prayer, meditation, or discussion.

While the devotional readings themselves need few additional words of introduction, it may be helpful to consider the following suggestions:

Take time for silence: Have one partner read the title and the few brief lines of introduction aloud. Then take a moment of silence to focus yourselves on the theme presented. You may want an additional period of silence after the responsive reading or during the prayer.

Take time for listening: Either partner may read the sentences in italic or those sentences which appear in roman type of the responsive reading. When it is not your turn to read, there may be a temptation to skim over your partner's lines, but make the effort to listen to each other. Try to read slowly. Pause slightly between the parts to give yourselves time to understand what you have read.

Take time for meditation and discussion: Some of the readings end with a section of questions for meditation and discussion. But even when specific suggestions are absent, take a moment after the responsive reading to think about and to discuss the Scripture passage presented. What does it mean to you? How does it affect your life? Use Bible dictionaries, commentaries, or other study resources if you wish. For additional assistance, some background information on the book of Matthew and a list of basic discussion questions for the readings appear in the final section of the book.

Take time for prayer: Before you pray, you may want to mention some specific prayer concerns. Take time to share your goals and dreams together. Encourage one another. Then pray together silently or conversationally, in your own words or in the words of the closing prayer where provided. Again, for extra help, some aids to sharing and praying together appear at the end of the book.

As these devotional readings are shared together, not all of the suggestions may be appropriate for your situation. Use the ones which best suit your needs, and leave the rest. Feel free to develop new alternatives, new readings, new prayers.

This book is only a starting place for joint times of devotion. It really cannot be anything more. True devotion is not a matter of reading words on a printed page; it is a matter of heart, mind, and soul. It is communication with God. As you listen, read, and talk together with your partner and with God, the Holy Spirit will be at work, deepening faith and friendship. Christ will be truly with you, "for where two or three are gathered in my name, there am I in the midst of them" (Matthew 18:20).

April Yamasaki

For whatever was written in former days was written for our instruction, that by steadfastness and by the encouragement of the scriptures we might have hope. May the God of steadfastness and encouragement grant you to live in such harmony with one another, in accord with Christ Jesus, that together you may with one voice glorify the God and Father of our Lord Jesus Christ.

Romans 15:4–6

God with Us 1

Introduction: We gather together to be with God, knowing that God is always with us. We gather together to speak with God, knowing that God longs to speak with us.

Reading: (Matthew 1:18-25)

Since the beginning of time, God has spoken to men and women in many different ways.

In dreams and visions, in the burning bush, in the still small voice, in the words of the prophets, God has reached out to people throughout history.

But then God spoke in a new and more complete way, for God spoke to the world in the life of Jesus Christ, the Word of God made flesh.

Now the birth of Jesus Christ took place in this way. When his mother Mary had been betrothed to Joseph, before they came together she was found to be with child of the Holy Spirit. (v. 18)

For Joseph, this was very troubling. Could he continue with his plan for marriage? Would he marry a woman expecting a child that was not his?

And her husband Joseph, being a just man and unwilling to put her to shame, resolved to divorce her quietly. (v. 19)

It was a difficult decision for Joseph to make: to continue with his marriage, or to break it off; to divorce Mary publicly or to leave her quietly. Yet as Joseph struggled with his questions, he was not alone.

But as he considered this, behold an angel of the Lord appeared to him in a dream, saying, "Joseph, son of David, do not fear to take Mary your wife, for that which is conceived in her is of the Holy Spirit; she will bear a son, and you shall call his name Jesus, for he will save his people from their sins." (vv. 20, 21)

As the Holy Spirit had been active in creation and throughout all of history, here again God was at work in a mighty way. Israel's long-awaited Messiah was coming into the world.

All this took place to fulfill what the Lord had spoken by the prophet: "Behold a virgin shall conceive and bear a son and his name shall be called Emmanuel" (which means God with us). (vv. 22, 23)

These words from the prophet Isaiah announced the new presence of God in the person of Jesus Christ.

When Joseph woke from sleep, he did as the angel of the Lord commanded him; he took his wife, but knew her not until she had borne a son; and he called his name Jesus. (vv. 24, 25)

God spoke to Joseph and Mary years ago, as they prepared to welcome Jesus into their home.

God speaks to us today, as we welcome Jesus to reign in our lives.

God was with Joseph years ago, as he struggled with his decision of marriage.

God is with us today, even as we struggle with our own decisions of life and work.

God was with Mary years ago, as she faced the days of waiting and wondering ahead of her.

God is with us today, even as we face the unknown future ahead of us.

Prayer: Thank you, God, for your active presence in our lives through Jesus, our Immanuel. Amen.

Preparing the Way 2

Introduction: God has prepared us for this time together.
Let us listen to the Word of God.

Reading: (Matthew 3:1–11)

For years God had been preparing the way for the coming Messiah.

God's prophet Micah spoke of Jesus' birth in Bethlehem.

God's prophet Jeremiah and others wrote of Jesus' tribe and family.

And when Jesus was finally ready to begin a public ministry, God sent yet another prophet to prepare the way.

In those days came John the Baptist, preaching in the wilderness of Judea, "Repent, for the kingdom of heaven is at hand." (vv. 1, 2)

John proclaimed the same message of repentance preached by the Old Testament prophets before him. In fact, those earlier prophets predicted John's own ministry.

For this is he who was spoken of by the prophet Isaiah when he said, "The voice of one crying in the wilderness: Prepare the way of the Lord, make his paths straight." (v. 3)

God also spoke of John through the prophet Malachi, saying, "Behold, I send my messenger to prepare the way before me." (Malachi 3:1a)

Now John wore a garment of camel's hair, and a leather girdle around his waist; and his food was locusts and wild honey. (v. 4)

John was a prophet prepared in the desert by God. He had a special mission to proclaim God's reign and to preach repentance to the people.

Then went out to him Jerusalem and all Judea and all the region about the Jordan, and they were baptized by him in the river Jordan, confessing their sins. (vv. 5, 6)

Even Pharisees and Sadducees came to the river for baptism. But John wanted to be sure that they understood this sign of repentance.

But when he saw many of the Pharisees and Sadducees coming for baptism, he said to them, "You brood of vipers! Who warned you to flee from the wrath to come?" (v. 7)

True repentance would mean turning from their old life of pride and living a new one of humility and service.

"Bear fruit that befits repentance, and do not presume to say to yourselves, 'We have Abraham as our father'; for I tell you, God is able from these stones to raise up children to Abraham." (vv. 8, 9)

John's message was one of judgment against those who refused to repent.

"Even now the axe is laid to the root of the trees; every tree therefore that does not bear good fruit is cut down and thrown into the fire." (v. 10)

But it was also a message of hope, for John declared the coming of Christ.

"I baptize you with water for repentance, but he who is coming after me is mightier than I, whose sandals I am not worthy to carry; he will baptize you with the Holy Spirit and with fire." (v. 11)

Prayer: As many of the people in the area of Jerusalem renewed their commitment to God when they heard John's message, may we also renew our commitment to God this day. Amen.

The Lamb of God 3

Introduction: Our gracious God, we confess that we have failed to be all that you have meant us to be. We have neglected the people and the tasks which you have entrusted to us. We have done things unworthy of your name. Forgive us and create a new spirit within us. In the name of Jesus, the Lamb of God that takes away the sin of the world. Amen.

Reading: (Matthew 3:13–17)

We know that we are not always faithful to God's call for justice, mercy, and humility.

Christ alone is the forever faithful Servant of God.

We know that we are not always true to God's call for righteousness.

Christ alone is the forever true Righteousness of God.

We know that we are not always committed to God's call for self-sacrifice.

Christ alone is the forever pure Lamb of God.

So when the sinless Christ came to John for baptism, John almost turned him away.

Then Jesus came from Galilee to the Jordan to John, to be baptized by him. John would have prevented him, saying, "I need to be baptized by you, and do you come to me?" (vv. 13, 14)

But this was a necessary first step in Jesus' public ministry. By his baptism, he identified with all of God's people and showed his own willingness to obey all of God's commands.

But Jesus answered him, "Let it be so now; for thus it is fitting for us to fulfill all righteousness." Then he consented. (v. 15)

God confirmed the appropriateness of Jesus' baptism by the visible descent of the Spirit and with a voice of affirmation.

And when Jesus was baptized, he went up immediately from the water, and behold, the heavens were opened and he saw the Spirit of God descending like a dove, and alighting on him; and lo, a voice from heaven, saying, "This is my beloved Son, with whom I am well pleased." (vv. 16, 17)

In spite of his own sinlessness, Jesus was unafraid to identify with people in need of repentance.

In his baptism, and throughout his entire ministry, he was unafraid for his own reputation.

He freely associated with tax collectors and prostitutes.

He freely touched those labeled unclean and spoke to those possessed by demons.

Like all of these people in need of repentance, we know we are not always faithful to God's call for justice, mercy, and humility, yet the forever faithful Servant of God stands with us in spite of our weakness.

We know we are not always true to God's call for righteousness, yet the forever true Righteousness of God reaches out to us in spite of our waywardness.

We know that we are not always committed to God's call for self-sacrifice, yet the forever pure Lamb of God sacrificed the glory of heaven to take on human flesh for our sake.

Prayer: Our merciful God, we thank you for your forgiveness and renewal. Grant us fresh grace to respond to your call. Amen.

Tempted As We Are 4

Introduction: For we have not a high priest who is unable to sympathize with our weaknesses, but one who in every respect has been tempted as we are, yet without sin. (Hebrews 4:15)

Reading: (Matthew (4:1–10)

We are tempted from without and from within, by the sights and sounds of the world around us, and by the longings of our own hearts.

We are tempted to be untrue to ourselves, to try to be someone or something that we are not.

We are tempted to be untrue to others, to label them, and to limit them for our own purposes and our own convenience.

We are tempted to be untrue to God, to deny God's claim on our lives and to refuse God's grace.

Such temptations are part of human life. They come to you and to me, even as they came to Jesus Christ.

Then Jesus was led up by the Spirit into the wilderness to be tempted by the devil. And he fasted forty days and forty nights, and afterward he was hungry. And the tempter came and said to him, "If you are the Son of God, command these stones to become loaves of bread." (vv. 1–3)

Jesus was tempted to perform a miracle to satisfy his own physical hunger, to misuse God's power for himself.

But he answered, "It is written, 'Man shall not live by bread alone, but by every word that proceeds from the mouth of God.' " (v. 4)

Jesus refused to break his fast at Satan's bidding. He trusted God to sustain both his physical and spiritual strength.

Then the devil took him to the holy city, and set him on the pinnacle of the temple, and said to him, "If you are the Son of God, throw yourself down; for it is written, 'He will give his angels charge of you,' and 'On their hands they will bear you up, lest you strike your foot against a stone.' " (vv. 5, 6)

Jesus was tempted to do something spectacular to prove God's care for him, to use God's power to call attention to himself.

Jesus said to him, "Again it is written, 'You shall not tempt the Lord your God.' " (v. 7)

Once again Jesus kept his faith in God. He knew better than to put God to the test so carelessly and needlessly.

Again, the devil took him to a very high mountain, and showed him all the kingdoms of the world, and the glory of them; and he said to him, "All these I will give you, if you will fall down and worship me." (vv. 8, 9)

Jesus was tempted to compromise his faith in God, to worship Satan in return for worldly power.

Then Jesus said to him, "Begone Satan! for it is written, 'You shall worship the Lord your God and him only shall you serve.' " (v. 10)

And so we pray for an undivided heart, O God, to worship you alone.

We pray for an honest intention to use your gifts and power in obedience to you alone.

We pray for an unwavering faith in your purposes, for you alone are God. Amen.

Meditation/Discussion: What specific things did Jesus say or do to overcome temptation? Can you use them in your own life? Why or why not?

The Beatitudes 5

Introduction: Our God, we thank you for the beatitudes, which reflect the perfection of your own character. As your disciples, may we make each of these qualities our own. Amen.

Reading: (Matthew 5:1–12)

Seeing the crowds, Jesus went up on the mountain, and when he sat down his disciples came to him. And he opened his mouth and taught them, saying: "Blessed are the poor in spirit, for theirs is the kingdom of heaven." (vv. 1–3)

Our God, teach us to be poor in spirit. Like the humble poor of the Old Testament, may we know our own helplessness and place all our trust in you.

"Blessed are those who mourn, for they shall be comforted." (v. 4)

Our God, teach us to mourn. May the sin and suffering of this world be our sorrow as it is yours.

"Blessed are the meek, for they shall inherit the earth." (v. 5)

Our God, teach us to be meek. May we be willing to accept our place as the children of God and to live accordingly in humility and gentleness with one another.

"Blessed are those who hunger and thirst for righteousness, for they shall be satisfied." (v. 6)

Our God, teach us to hunger and thirst for righteousness. May our longing to do your will find expression in daily obedience.

"Blessed are the merciful, for they shall obtain mercy." (v. 7)

Our God, teach us to be merciful. May we be generous and forgiving in spirit, ready to encourage and to help one another.

"Blessed are the pure in heart, for they shall see God." (v. 8)

Our God, teach us to be pure in heart. May even our most secret thoughts honor and glorify your name.

"Blessed are the peacemakers, for they shall be called children of God." (v. 9)

Our God, teach us to be peacemakers as true sons and daughters. May we be reconciled to you and to one another in the human family, as agents of reconciliation in this troubled world.

"Blessed are those who are persecuted for righteousness' sake, for theirs is the kingdom of heaven. Blessed are you when men revile you and persecute you and utter all kinds of evil against you falsely on my account. Rejoice and be glad, for your reward is great in heaven, for so men persecuted the prophets who were before you." (vv. 10–12)

Our God, teach us to find our joy in you. May it make us steadfast under persecution and able to stand firm amid insults and false accusations.

Blessed are those who practice daily each spiritual quality and receive gladly each special blessing.

Our God, we do not seek these qualities for the sake of the blessings, but because we want to follow you. Amen.

Meditation/Discussion: With which beatitude do you identify the most closely? With which beatitude do you identify the least?

We Are Salt and Light 6

Introduction: We were created in the image of God, who knows us through and through, even better than we know ourselves.

Reading: (Matthew 5:13–16)

Sometimes I wonder what kind of person I really am. One day I feel confident and ready to face the world. Another day I am fearful and filled with self-doubts.

One day I am certain of my goals and purpose in life. Another day I wonder just what I'm doing here.

Some days I can't understand my own feelings.

Some days I don't even know how I feel.

So then, who am I? A contradiction of sorts. A puzzle. I am confident and fearful, at times unable to understand myself or to identify my own feelings. Who am I?

You are the salt of the earth; (v. 13a)

I am a grain of salt in this world, for I have known the taste of God's grace.

But if salt has lost its taste, how shall its saltness be restored? It is no longer good for anything except to be thrown out and trodden underfoot by men. (v. 13b)

But if I lose that flavor, how can I add a taste of God's grace to the world? How can I be salt to others if I am not alive to God's presence?

You are the light of the world. (v. 14a)

I am a ray of light in this world, for I have known the spark of God's love.

A city set on a hill cannot be hid. Nor do men light a lamp and put it under a bushel, but on a stand, and it gives light to all in the house. (vv. 14b, 15)

But if I hide that light, how can I add a spark of God's love to the world? How can I be light to others if I hide myself away?

Let your light so shine before men, that they may see your good works and give glory to your Father who is in heaven. (v. 16)

You too are the salt of the earth.

I am in the world, but not of it. I can make a difference in this world, for I can add a taste of God's grace to it.

You too are the light of the world.

I am in the world, but not of it. I can make a difference in this world, for I can add a spark of God's love to it.

It is a high calling to be salt and light. It seems almost impossible to be so pure and true.

Yet if we follow Christ, the true Salt and the true Light of the world, we can help others in giving glory to our God who is in heaven.

So let us follow Christ, and be salt and light wherever God has placed us in this world.

Glory be to God our Creator, to Christ our Savior, and to the Holy Spirit our Guide. Amen.

Meditation/Discussion: Identify some situations in the world today that need the salt of healing and the light of understanding. How might you be salt and light in those areas?

The Law and the Prophets 7

Introduction: We have not received a spirit of bondage, but a spirit of freedom. We have not received a spirit of fear, but a spirit of grace. Amen.

Reading: (Matthew 5:17–20)

In Jesus Christ, we are set free from the bondage of sin and the fear of judgment. In Christ we know the fullness of God's freedom and grace.

But freedom is not license, and grace is not lawlessness. Even Jesus spoke highly of the Old Testament law and the prophets.

Think not that I have come to abolish the law and the prophets; I have come not to abolish them but to fulfill them. (v. 17)

Jesus upheld the Old Testament law as an expression of God's will.

For truly, I say to you, till heaven and earth pass away, not an iota, not a dot, will pass from the law until all is accomplished. (v. 18)

Jesus realized that the law expressed God's enduring intention for righteous living.

Whoever then relaxes one of the least of these commandments and teaches men so, shall be called least in the kingdom of heaven; but he who does them and teaches them shall be called great in the kingdom of heaven. (v. 19)

Jesus recognized the place of the law even in the lives of his own followers, for the same love of God and neighbor required by the old law is the law of love in God's new kingdom.

For I tell you, unless your righteousness exceeds that of the scribes and Pharisees, you will never enter the kingdom of heaven. (v. 20)

In fact, Jesus expected his followers to be even more faithful to God's law of love than the scribes and Pharisees.

They said whoever kills shall be liable to judgment.

But Jesus said whoever is angry with another shall be liable to judgment.

They said not to commit adultery.

But Jesus said not even to look lustfully at another.

They said that whoever divorces his wife must give her a certificate of divorce.

But Jesus said that whoever divorces his wife, except on the ground of unchastity, makes her turn to adultery.

They said to keep the oaths which you swear.

But Jesus said to keep your word, whether it be a simple yes or no.

They said to limit retaliation to "an eye for an eye and a tooth for a tooth."

But Jesus said to return evil with good.

They said to love your neighbor.

But Jesus said to love even your enemies and to pray for your persecutors.

They could not keep the law of God.

But Jesus lived it to the fullest.

Prayer: O God of freedom and grace, thank you for our new life in Christ. Teach us to walk in your way, we pray. Amen.

The Disciples' Prayer 8

Introduction: Our God, forgive us when our prayers become mere words recited without true meaning. It's all too easy for us to fall into such carelessness with a familiar passage of Scripture like the "Lord's Prayer." Help us to offer it to you today with new intention and fresh commitment. Amen.

Reading: (Matthew 6:5–13)

And when you pray, you must not be like the hypocrites; for they love to stand and pray in the synagogues and at the street corners, that they may be seen by men. Truly, I say to you, they have received their reward. (v. 5)

Forgive us, our God, when we pray with false motives and proud hearts. May we grow in sincerity and a true humility.

But when you pray, go into your room and shut the door and pray to your Father who is in secret; and your Father who sees in secret will reward you. (v. 6)

Forgive us, our God, when we pray with the hope of gaining human praise. May we commune with you in the private depths of our own being, and learn to meet you there.

And in praying do not heap up empty phrases as the Gentiles do; for they think that they will be heard for their many words. (v. 7)

Forgive us, our God, when we doubt your attention to our prayers. May we remember that you hear even those silent petitions we cannot express.

Do not be like the Gentiles, for your Father knows what you need before you ask him. (v. 8)

Forgive us, our God, when we lack faith in the riches of your wisdom. May we renew our trust in you, for you know us even more thoroughly than we know ourselves.

Pray then like this: Our Father who art in heaven, Hallowed be thy name. (v. 9)

We praise you, our God, for you are a personal God and worthy of all honor and all glory.

Thy kingdom come, Thy will be done, On earth as it is in heaven. (v. 10)

We praise you, our God, for you call us as active participants in your kingdom, to seek your reign of peace and justice in all the earth.

Give us this day our daily bread; (v. 11)

We praise you, our God, for you satisfy all our needs, that we might also share what we have with others.

And forgive us our debts, As we also have forgiven our debtors; (v. 12)

We praise you, our God, for you forgive all our shortcomings, that we might also forgive one another.

And lead us not into temptation, But deliver us from evil. (v. 13)

We praise you, our God, for you guide us through every temptation and trial and watch over us until the end.

For thine is the kingdom, the power, and the glory.

For ever and ever. Amen.

Meditation/Discussion: Think about one phrase of the disciples' prayer. What does it say about God? What does it require of you?

Called to Serve God 9

Introduction: Listen to the silence. Can you hear the voice of God? Closer than the sound of our own breathing, more insistent than the beat of our own hearts, God calls us. Listen.

Reading: (Matthew 6:19–24)

re crowded with many voices.

tplace calls us to set our sights on its

lace calls us to climb its ladder of success.

unity calls us to devote ourselves to social

h calls us to support its worship and
ies.

circle calls us to commit ourselves to family
and friends.

But Jesus calls us to love and serve God above all these things.

Do not lay up for yourselves treasures on earth, where moth and rust consume and where thieves break in and steal, but lay up for yourselves treasure in heaven, where neither moth nor rust consumes and where thieves do not break in and steal. For where your treasure is, there will your heart be also. (vv. 19–21)

Do not be concerned about acquiring the temporary pleasures and possessions of this world. Rather value the ever-lasting life and work of the kingdom of God, for whatever stands at the center of your life will order your priorities.

The eye is the lamp of the body. So, if your eye is sound, your whole body will be full of light; but if your eye is not sound, your whole body will be full of darkness. If then the light in you is darkness, how great is the darkness! (vv. 22, 23)

The eye gives sight to the body. But if the eye does not focus on what it sees, the body will lack good direction. In the same way, if we want clear purpose and real direction in life, we must learn to focus our attention on just one thing.

No one can serve two masters; for either he will hate the one and love the other, or he will be devoted to the one and despise the other. (v. 24a)

No one can give a single-minded commitment to two different things. To give ourselves wholeheartedly to God, we must give up all others.

You cannot serve God and mammon. (v. 24b)

We cannot give wholehearted devotion to both God and money.

We cannot give wholehearted devotion to both God and our own prestige and reputation.

Even our work in the community, the church, and among our own family and friends must be set in relation to God, for even a good work can become a false master and a false god.

But there is one God, whose face we seek.

There is one God, whose voice we long to hear. Listen.

Prayer: Our God, as we try to sort out the many voices in our world, keep us single-minded in our commitment to you. Order our priorities according to your will, we pray. Amen.

Be Anxious for Nothing 10

Introduction: O God, the source of life and the giver of every good thing, be with us today as always and make us receptive to your word. Amen.

Reading: (Matthew 6:25–34)

Ours is an anxious age and full of uncertainties.

We are anxious about the future. Where will we be tomorrow? Will there be a tomorrow?

We are anxious about the past. Did we say the right thing yesterday? Did we make the right decision?

We are anxious about the present. Are we in good health? Do we have friends?

Sometimes our anxieties keep us awake at night.

Sometimes our anxieties even prevent us from performing our daily tasks.

But if God has given us life itself, then surely God can preserve our future, forgive our past, and provide for our present.

Therefore I tell you, do not be anxious about your life, what you shall eat or what you shall drink, nor about your body, what you shall put on. Is not life more than food, and the body more than clothing? (v. 25)

Anxiety is unnecessary and unreasonable.

Look at the birds of the air: they neither sow nor reap nor gather into barns, and yet your heavenly Father feeds them. Are you not of more value than they? (v. 26)

Anxiety cannot give us a longer life.

And which of you by being anxious can add one cubit to his span of life? (v. 27)

Anxiety cannot give us a better life.

And why are you anxious about clothing? Consider the lilies of the field, how they grow; they neither toil nor spin; yet I tell you, even Solomon in all his glory was not arrayed like one of these. But if God so clothes the grass of the field, which today is alive and tomorrow is thrown into the oven will he not much more clothe you, O you of little faith? (vv. 28–30)

Anxiety shows a lack of trust in God. It has no power to accomplish the things we worry about.

Therefore do not be anxious, saying, 'What shall we eat?' or 'What shall we drink?' or 'What shall we wear?' (v. 31)

Let us replace anxiety with faith that God will satisfy our needs.

For the Gentiles seek all these things; and your heavenly Father knows that you need them all. (v. 32)

Let us replace anxiety with setting proper goals.

But seek first his kingdom and his righteousness, and all these things shall be yours as well. (v. 33)

Let us replace anxiety with living one day at a time.

Therefore do not be anxious about tomorrow, for tomorrow will be anxious for itself. Let the day's own trouble be sufficient for the day. (v. 34)

Meditation/Discussion: How do you respond to anxiety in your own life? Are you anxious over anything today? Why or why not? Discuss this with your partner and then pray together.

Free From Condemnation 11

Introduction: God bids us welcome today, just as we are—with all our joys and sorrows, with all our fears and failures. Thanks be to God.

Reading: (Matthew 7:1-5)

Thanks be to God for the welcome we receive.

For all our imperfections, God is ready to accept us.

Thanks be to God for the mercy we experience.

For all our flaws and faults, God is ready to forgive us.

Thanks be to God for the freedom we enjoy.

For all our past, God is ready to give us a new start.

Jesus himself said that he did not come to judge the world, but to save it.

He did not come to condemn the world, but to reconcile it to God.

But in spite of the great mercy we've received, we have yet to learn more fully how to pass it on to those around us.

We have yet to learn the patience and generous grace of God.

We criticize each other for our imperfections.

We blame each other for our flaws.

We condemn each other for our faults.

But if God, who is perfect, does not condemn us, who are we to condemn one another?

Judge not, that you be not judged. (v. 1)

When we stand in judgment over another person, we cut ourselves off from the mercy of God.

For with the judgment you pronounce you will be judged, and the measure you give will be the measure you get. (v. 2)

When we stand in judgment over another person, we are blinded to the flaws in our own lives and personalities.

Why do you see the speck that is in your brother's eye, but do not notice the log that is in your own eye? (v. 3)

When we stand in judgment over another person, we act with false pride.

Or how can you say to your brother, "Let me take the speck out of your eye," when there is the log in your own eye? (v. 4)

When we stand in judgment over another person, we put our time and energy to the wrong task.

You hypocrite, first take the log out of your own eye, and then you will see clearly to take the speck out of your brother's eye. (v. 5)

Then let us set each other free from any condemnation.

Thanks be to God for the freedom we enjoy.

Then let us give each other mercy in our weakness.

Thanks be to God for the mercy we experience.

Then let us welcome each other as God has welcomed us.

Thanks be to God for the welcome we receive.

Prayer: In Christ, there is no condemnation. Thanks be to God. Amen.

Persistent in Prayer 12

Introduction: Rejoice always, pray constantly, give thanks in all circumstances; for this is the will of God in Christ Jesus for you. (1 Thessalonians 5:16–18)

Reading: (Matthew 7:7–11)

I know that I need to pray more often, but sometimes I feel as if I'm just talking to myself.

I know that I need to pray more often, but sometimes I feel that if God already knows everything about me, prayer has no purpose.

I know that I need to pray more often, but sometimes I feel my prayers don't make any difference to my life or to those around me.

I know that I need to pray more often, but sometimes I feel afraid that God won't answer me.

But prayer is more than trying to talk to God.

It is learning to listen to God.

Prayer is more than telling God about myself.

It is learning from God who I am and who I can be.

Prayer is more than trying to change God or other people.

It is learning to be changed by God, so that I can take part in God's work in the world.

Prayer is more than getting the answers I want from God.

It is learning to ask the right questions.

So let us be persistent in prayer, for God will surely meet us.

Ask, and it will be given you; seek, and you will find; knock, and it will be opened to you. (v. 7)

Let us be faithful in prayer, for God will surely answer us.

For every one who asks receives, and he who seeks finds, and to him who knocks it will be opened. (v. 8)

Let us be confident in prayer, for God will surely be good to us.

Or what man of you, if his son asks him for bread, will give him a stone? Or if he asks for a fish, will give him a serpent? If you then, who are evil, know how to give good gifts to your children, how much more will your Father who is in heaven give good things to those who ask him! (vv. 9–11)

Thank you, God, for prayer. Though we may not always feel close to you when we pray, we know that you hear us.

Thank you, God, for prayer. Though you already know everything about us, there is still reason to pray, for it strengthens our relationship with you.

Thank you, God, for prayer. Though we may not always recognize the results of our prayers, they make us grow in our relationship with you and challenge us to join in your work.

Thank you, God, for prayer. Though you don't always answer us in the way we expect, we know that you always act for our good. Amen.

Meditation/Discussion: Think of a specific situation in your own life. Can you rejoice over it, pray for it, and give thanks to God because of it? Why or why not?

Beware of False Prophets 13

Introduction: Beloved, do not believe every spirit, but test the spirits to see whether they are of God; for many false prophets have gone out into the world. (1 John 4:1)

Reading: (Matthew 7:15–23)

I thought Jesus taught his disciples not to judge one another.

He said, "Judge not, that you be not judged." (Matthew 7:1).

Yet his disciple John taught the church to test the prophets.

He said, "Test the spirits to see whether they are of God." (1 John 4:1)

It sounds like a contradiction at first, but there's actually a big difference between judging and testing.

When we judge people, we criticize them and condemn them. But when we test people, we weigh the truth of their teaching.

We cannot judge one another, not even those who call themselves prophets. Judgment belongs to God.

But we must test these prophets, for we need to accept the true and reject the false.

Jesus even said false prophets may appear to be a part of the Christian community, but they are actually from outside of it and threaten our life with God.

Beware of false prophets, who come to you in sheep's clothing but inwardly are ravenous wolves. (v. 15)

Jesus said false prophets may sound like true prophets, but they prove themselves false by the way they live.

You will know them by their fruits. Are grapes gathered from thorns, or figs from thistles? So every sound tree bears good fruit, but the bad tree bears evil fruit. A sound tree cannot bear evil fruit, nor can a bad tree bear good fruit. (vv. 16–18)

Jesus said false prophets may call themselves prophets, but they stand under judgment for they do not keep God's will.

Every tree that does not bear good fruit is cut down and thrown into the fire. Thus you will know them by their fruits. (vv. 19, 20)

Jesus said false prophets may pay lip service to God, but they are not really God's servants.

Not every one who says to me, "Lord, Lord," shall enter the kingdom of heaven, but he who does the will of my Father who is in heaven. (v. 21)

Jesus said false prophets may even perform spectacular works, but they are far from God.

On that day many will say to me, "Lord, Lord, did we not prophesy in your name, and cast out demons in your name, and do many mighty works in your name?" And then will I declare to them, "I never knew you; depart from me, you evildoers." (vv. 22, 23)

Until that day, God grant us wisdom to distinguish truth from falsehood.

Until that day, God grant us courage to confront lip service with life service, and falsehood with truth. Amen.

Meditation/Discussion: What instances of "lip service" and "life service" can you identify in the world today and in your own life?

A Centurion Faith 14

Introduction: Our God, we come to you with all of our doubts, discouragements, and uncertainties. Yet in spite of them all, we will cling to you. Help our unbelief, we pray. Amen.

Reading: (Matthew 8:5-13)

In the face of doubt, we dare to believe.

We believe in God, who creates and sustains all things.

In the face of discouragement, we dare to hope.

We hope in Christ, who seeks and saves the lost.

In the face of uncertainty, we dare to have faith.

We have faith in the Holy Spirit, who comforts and uplifts us.

Faith believes and hopes in what is true, even though it cannot be seen.

Faith brings its need to God, even when it is almost beyond hope.

As Jesus entered Capernaum, a centurion came forward to him, beseeching him and saying, "Lord, my servant is lying paralyzed at home, in terrible distress." (vv. 5, 6)

Faith finds God ready to meet its need, even before it makes its request.

And he said to him, "I will come and heal him." (v. 7)

Faith trusts in the power of God, even though it is conscious of its own unworthiness.

But the centurion answered him, "Lord, I am not worthy to have you come under my roof; but only say the word, and my servant will be healed. For I am a man under authority with soldiers under me; and I say to one, 'Go,' and he goes, and to another, 'Come,' and he comes, and to my slave, 'Do this,' and he does it." (vv. 8, 9)

Faith gains favor with God, wherever it is found.

When Jesus heard him, he marvelled, and said to those who followed him, "Truly, I say to you, not even in Israel have I found such faith. I tell you, many will come from east and west and sit at table with Abraham, Isaac, and Jacob in the kingdom of heaven, while the sons of the kingdom will be thrown into the outer darkness; there men will weep and gnash their teeth." (vv. 10–12)

Faith finds God true in word and deed.

And to the centurion Jesus said, "Go; be it done for you as you have believed." And the servant was healed at that very moment. (v. 13)

The faith of the centurion was answered by the faithfulness of God.

So strengthen our faith in you, O God.

The hope of the centurion was fulfilled by the word of God.

So strengthen our hope in you, O God.

The trust of the centurion was confirmed by the power of God.

So strengthen our trust in you, O God. Amen.

Meditation/Discussion: Where is there doubt, discouragement, or uncertainty in your life today? How can the example of the centurion's faith help you in dealing with these?

The First Step 15

Introduction: Our God, we thank you for the way you have led us in the past— step by step toward you, and step by step toward each other. Thank you for always being at our side. Amen.

Reading: (Matthew 9:9–13)

For most of us, it isn't easy to admit our need for God.

Like the rest of our western society, we tend to exaggerate our own self-sufficiency.

We often over-estimate our independence.

We rely more on our own work than on the providence of God.

Yet, we are unable to maintain our self-sufficiency, for that would be a lie.

We are unable to maintain a complete independence, for that would be isolation.

We are unable to rely completely on our own efforts, for there is much in life beyond our control.

Then why is it so hard to admit our needs, even to ourselves? It is the truth.

Then why are we so afraid to admit we need God? It is the first step toward discipleship.

As Jesus passed on from there, he saw a man called Matthew sitting at the tax office; and he said to him, "Follow me." And he rose and followed him. (v. 9)

Matthew made that first step toward discipleship. He knew he needed God, so when he heard Jesus' call, he was ready to respond to it. Then he prepared a great feast for Jesus at his own home.

And as he sat at table in the house, behold, many tax collectors and sinners came and sat down with Jesus and his disciples. (v. 10)

These tax collectors and sinners had nothing to lose in admitting their need for God, for they were already despised by their own society.

And when the Pharisees saw this, they said to his disciples, "Why does your teacher eat with tax collectors and sinners?" (v. 11)

The self-righteous Pharisees did not approve of Jesus' willing association with such social outcasts. When Jesus heard their criticism, he could not let it go unanswered.

But when he heard it, he said, "Those who are well have no need of a physician, but those who are sick. Go and learn what this means, 'I desire mercy, and not sacrifice.' For I came not to call the righteous, but sinners." (vv. 12, 13)

Jesus knew that the Pharisees' refusal to admit their need for God prevented them from hearing God's message.

In the same way, if we are busy with our own self-righteousness, we cannot hear God's call to sinners.

If we are preoccupied with proving our own independence, we cannot accept God's invitation to be a new community.

If we are relying on our own strength, we cannot be open to God's grace.

Prayer: Our God, thank you for calling us to yourself in the person of Jesus Christ. May we hear that call today even more clearly and join together in love and service to you. In the name of Jesus, who satisfies all our longings. Amen.

All Things Made New 16

Introduction: To the distressed, God is the one Joy. To the bound, God is the great Liberator. To the weary, God is the new Life. Glory be to God. Amen.

Reading: (Matthew 9:14–17)

The law of Moses has always occupied a central position in the Jewish religion.

But during the time of Jesus, the original intent of much of the law had been buried under a host of regulations.

The keeping of the Sabbath was meant to be a remembrance of God as Creator and Deliverer.

But for some it had become a preoccupation with themselves and their own behavior.

The observance of religious cleanliness was meant to be a mark of purity.

But for some it had become a barrier to love and service.

The regular fasts were meant to express true humility before God.

But for some they had become occasions for human pride.

To this spirit of legalism, Jesus brought a new freedom from the old distorted rituals.

To this dry tradition he brought true humility, purity, and godliness.

But the religious Jews did not understand Jesus' new way of living. Even the disciples of John the Baptist questioned his teaching and practice.

Then the disciples of John came to him, saying, "Why do we and the Pharisees fast, but your disciples do not fast?" (v. 14)

John's disciples expected Jesus and his disciples to practice the accepted religious rituals of the day. But Jesus' good news required a new way of living.

And Jesus said to them, "Can the wedding guests mourn as long as the bridegroom is with them? The days will come, when the bridegroom is taken away from them, and then they will fast." (v. 15)

In Jesus Christ, God is present with us. It's a cause for celebration rather than mourning.

"And no one puts a piece of unshrunk cloth on an old garment, for the patch tears away from the old garment, and a worse tear is made." (v. 16)

In Jesus Christ, God's true righteousness lives. It breaks away from empty legalism.

"Neither is new wine put into old wineskins; if it is, the skins burst, and the wine is spilled, and the skins are destroyed; but new wine is put into fresh wineskins, and so both are preserved." (v. 17)

In Jesus Christ, God's new covenant is proclaimed. It cannot be contained by the rituals of the past.

Then glory be to God for the new joy of God's presence.

Glory be to God for the new freedom from legalism.

Glory be to God for the new life in Jesus Christ.

Meditation/Discussion: In what ways has God brought newness to your lives? What old idea or practice has God replaced or transformed?

Enduring to the End 17

Introduction: Sometimes we are tempted to be silent when we should speak, to be still when we should act. Give us courage instead to speak and act according to your Spirit. Amen.

Reading: (Matthew 10:16–22)

It isn't easy to be a Christian these days.

It hasn't been easy to be a Christian any day.

Some people misunderstand my faith.

They do not understand commitment to Christ.

Some people discourage my faith.

They would rather that you be one of the crowd.

Some people criticize my faith.

They do not accept God's claim on our lives.

But Jesus never said the Christian life would be easy. In fact, he warned his disciples of the dangers they would face.

Behold, I send you out as sheep in the midst of wolves; so be wise as serpents and innocent as doves. (v. 16)

He warned his disciples of persecution from religious and government authorities.

Beware of men; for they will deliver you up to councils, and flog you in their synagogues, and you will be dragged before governors and kings for my sake, to bear testimony before them and the Gentiles. (vv. 17, 18)

Yet in spite of this coming persecution, the disciples did not need to be anxious, for the Spirit of God would be with them.

When they deliver you up, do not be anxious how you are to speak or what you are to say; for what you are to say will be given to you in that hour; for it is not you who speak, but the Spirit of your Father speaking through you. (vv. 19, 20)

In spite of the coming rejection from their own families, they did not need to be anxious, for endurance and deliverance would go hand in hand.

Brother will deliver up brother to death, and the father his child, and children will rise against parents and have them put to death; and you will be hated by all for my name's sake. But he who endures to the end will be saved. (vv. 21, 22)

Jesus himself was misunderstood. Some people did not see him for who he really was.

He was a man despised and rejected by men; a man of sorrows, and acquainted with grief; and as one from whom men hide their faces he was despised, and we esteemed him not. (Isaiah 53:5)

Jesus himself faced discouragement and criticism. Some people did not accept him for who he really was.

Surely he has borne our griefs and carried our sorrows; yet we esteemed him stricken, smitten by God, and afflicted. (Isaiah 53:4)

So, then, the Christian life is not an easy one, for we servants are not above our master, who suffered and endured to the end.

Yet as we follow in Jesus' steps with patience, endurance, and steadfast faith, God is also faithful to deliver us.

Meditation/Discussion: In what ways do you feel people misunderstand, discourage, or criticize your faith? Pray about these together.

The Sword of Commitment 18

Introduction: Our God, we thank you for drawing us to yourself. Deepen our commitment to you and to each other as we meet again today. Amen.

Reading: (Matthew 10:34–39)

I thought Jesus was supposed to be the prince of peace. Did the angels not proclaim peace to the earth on the night of his birth?

Indeed peace is God's intention toward the earth and to all who dwell within it.

Did the apostle Paul not say that we have peace with God through Christ?

Indeed peace comes through Christ, who reconciles us to God.

Did Jesus not say, "Peace I leave with you"? (John 14:27)

Indeed peace is ours even in the face of anxiety and fear.

Yet Jesus warned his disciples against misunderstanding the kind of peace he could give them.

Do not think that I have come to bring peace on earth; I have not come to bring peace, but a sword. (v. 34)

The sword of commitment draws a line of division between those who follow Jesus and those who choose to go their own way. It causes division even between the closest of family members.

For I have come to set a man against his father, and a daughter against her mother, and a daughter-in-law against her mother-in-law; and a man's foes will be those of his own household. (vv. 35, 36)

The sword of commitment causes division even in the disciples' own hearts as they struggle to love God above all and to follow Christ alone.

He who loves father or mother more than me is not worthy of me; and he who loves son or daughter more than me is not worthy of me; and he who does not take his cross and follow me is not worthy of me. (vv. 37, 38)

Those who put themselves and their own families first will ultimately lose their lives. But those who commit themselves wholeheartedly to God will find abundant life.

He who finds his life will lose it, and he who loses his life for my sake will find it. (v. 39)

If we follow Christ we will face indifference and even hostility from family, friends, and acquaintances.

Yet we will know peace with God.

If we follow Christ, we will face temptations and difficult decisions.

Yet in spite of spiritual struggle, we will know the peace of inner conviction.

Grant us the courage, O God, to take up our cross.

It is the cross of walking with Christ even in the face of opposition from other people.

Grant us the strength, O God, to carry our cross.

It is the cross of Christ-like servanthood even in the face of opposition from our own hearts. Amen.

Meditation/Discussion: Where has the sword of commitment struck in your life? Can you see peace there as well?

A Holy Rest 19

Introduction: This is a time to cease all striving and busy thought. It is a time of worship and holy rest.

Reading: (Matthew 11:28-30)

In the days of Jesus' life on earth, the orthodox Jews had very little rest from religious duties.

There were public sacrifices given throughout the year, as well as private sacrifices for Passover, for child-birth, for cleansing from leprosy, and for many other occasions.

There were regulations about keeping the Sabbath and tithing.

There were rituals of fasting and handwashing.

In fact, there were so many laws that Jesus rebuked the scribes and Pharisees for laying such heavy and unnecessary burdens on the people.

And to those who labored to keep the law and who were weighted down with its demands, Jesus issued this invitation.

Come to me, all who labor and are heavy laden, and I will give you rest. (v. 28)

In the kingdom of God there is rest for those weary of legalism, for those tired of striving to meet endless lists of rules and regulations.

Take my yoke upon you, and learn from me; for I am gentle and lowly in heart, and you will find rest for your souls. (v. 29)

In the kingdom of God there is rest in the compassionate heart of Christ. Yet this rest is not mere idleness or careless living. It is a commitment of love and service taught by the one who loved and served God with his whole life.

For my yoke is easy, and my burden is light. (v. 30)

In the kingdom of God the yoke is easy, for Jesus himself wears it. The burden is light, for Jesus himself bears it up.

So come to Jesus, all who labor and are heavy laden, and God will give you rest.

We come, having labored too long in our own insufficient strength.

And God renews us for love and service.

We come, burdened with guilt, both true and false, for sins both real and imagined.

And God grants us pardon for our debts and release from false guilt.

We come, weighed down with responsibilities and obligations, with fears and doubts about ourselves and each other.

And God grants us fresh vision and further faith.

We come, O God, ready to learn from you. Teach us the gentleness of Jesus who healed the sick and welcomed the poor.

We come, O God, ready to learn from you. Teach us the humility of Jesus who counted tax gatherers and prostitutes among his friends.

We come, O God, ready for the rest that only you can give. Amen.

Meditation/Discussion: How do you discern the difference between legalism and obedience to God? Between idleness and holy rest?

Our God Reigns 20

Introduction: Let us direct our thoughts to the authority of our great God.

Reading: (Matthew 12:9–21)

Our God reigns over heaven and earth.

Through the living Word they were created, and to God they give their praise.

Our God reigns over every living thing.

By the Living Spirit they draw each breath, and to God they owe their lives.

And yet during Jesus' earthly ministry, God's reign met opposition from the religious establishment.

And Jesus went on from there, and entered their synagogue. And behold, there was a man with a withered hand. And they asked him, "Is it lawful to heal on the sabbath?" so that they might accuse him. (vv. 9, 10)

But Jesus knew what was in the Pharisees' hearts, and he gave them an answer based on their own law.

He said to them, "What man of you, if he has one sheep and it falls into a pit on the sabbath, will not lay hold of it and lift it out? Of how much more value is a man than a sheep! So it is lawful to do good on the sabbath." (vv. 11, 12)

The Pharisees were more concerned about their own traditions than about human need. But Jesus turned those values around.

Then he said to the man, "Stretch out your hand." And the man stretched it out, and it was restored, whole like the other. (v. 13)

The Pharisees would not acknowledge Jesus' authority over the observance of Sabbath regulations. They could not see beyond their own status and self-righteousness.

But the Pharisees went out and took counsel against him, how to destroy him. (v. 14)

Jesus knew full well what the Pharisees were planning, but it was not yet time for the final confrontation.

Jesus, aware of this, withdrew from there. And many followed him, and he healed them all, and ordered them not to make him known. This was to fulfill what was spoken by the prophet Isaiah: "Behold, my servant whom I have chosen, my beloved with whom my soul is well pleased. I will put my Spirit upon him, and he shall proclaim justice to the Gentiles. He will not wrangle or cry aloud, nor will any one hear his voice in the streets; he will not break a bruised reed or quench a smoldering wick, till he brings justice to victory; and in his name will the Gentiles hope." (vv. 15-21)

Our God reigns over both Jew and Gentile.

In Jesus, the Jews may find fulfillment of all God's promises, and in him the Gentiles may share God's grace.

Our God reigns over human tradition.

In God's economy, human need transcends religious custom, and the sabbath is a time for wholeness.

Our God reigns over all things visible and invisible.

Prayer: Our God, we acknowledge your reign in our lives and in the world around us. May we learn to live as true citizens of your kingdom. Amen.

Forgiveness with God 21

Introduction: But there is forgiveness with thee, that thou mayest be feared. (Psalm 130:4)

Reading: (Matthew 12:22-32)

God extends forgiveness to all of us and refuses no one.

God bears the pain of our sins and demands no payment.

God forgives our sins completely and remembers them no more.

God's forgiveness is for all people, for all their sins, for all time.

Yet there is a kind of hardness of heart that even God's forgiveness cannot reach.

One day Jesus warned some Pharisees about this very thing. It all began when he restored sight and speech to a man possessed by demons.

Then a blind and dumb demoniac was brought to him, and he healed him, so that the dumb man spoke and saw. And all the people were amazed, and said, "Can this be the Son of David?" But when the Pharisees heard it they said, "It is only by Beelzebul, the prince of demons, that this man casts out demons." (vv. 22-24)

But the accusation of these Pharisees was not logical. The forces of evil do not work to defeat themselves.

Knowing their thoughts, he said to them, "Every kingdom divided against itself is laid waste, and no city or house divided against itself will stand; and if Satan casts out Satan, he is divided against himself; how then will his kingdom stand?" (vv. 25, 26)

The accusation of these Pharisees was not consistent. The Jews themselves claimed to cast out demons by the power of God.

"And if I cast out demons by Beelzebul, by whom do your sons cast them out? Therefore they shall be your judges." (v. 27)

The accusation of these Pharisees denied the truth. Jesus' exercise of power spelled the defeat of the forces of evil.

"But if it is by the Spirit of God that I cast out demons, then the kingdom of God has come upon you. Or how can one enter a strong man's house and plunder his goods, unless he first binds the strong man? Then indeed he may plunder his house." (vv. 28, 29)

Jesus' argument demanded a response from his hearers. They could not remain neutral.

"He who is not with me is against me, and he who does not gather with me scatters." (v. 30)

Jesus went on to warn these Pharisees against their rejection of God's power at work in him. Repeated refusal to recognize God's Spirit would render them unable to accept God's forgiveness at all.

"Therefore I tell you, every sin and blasphemy will be forgiven men, but the blasphemy against the Spirit will not be forgiven." (v. 31)

Repeated refusal to accept the power at work in Christ is even more serious than rejecting Christ's own person.

"And whoever says a word against the Son of man will be forgiven; but whoever speaks against the Holy Spirit will not be forgiven, either in this age or in the age to come." (v. 32)

Prayer: Thank you, God, for the forgiveness you extend to all who need it. Please keep us from taking your great mercy for granted. Amen.

The Sower and the Soils 22

Introduction: O God of heaven and earth, plant in us your Spirit and patient harvest reap. Amen.

Reading: (Matthew 13:1-9)

That same day Jesus went out of the house and sat beside the sea. (v. 1)

But the people would not let Jesus spend this time alone.

And great crowds gathered about him, so that he got into a boat and sat there; and the whole crowd stood on the beach. (v. 2)

And Jesus had compassion on the people and taught them about the kingdom of God.

And he told them many things in parables, saying: "A sower went out to sow." (v. 3)

The sower is anyone who proclaims the good news of the kingdom among the people. It might be a preacher or a teacher speaking to a crowd, or you or me in conversation with a friend, or Jesus himself speaking to the multitudes who flocked to hear him.

"And as he sowed some seeds fell along the path, and the birds came and devoured them." (v. 4)

Some people who hear the good news of the kingdom do not understand it. Their hearts and their minds are as hard as a well-traveled pathway, and they cannot accept the good news for what it is.

"Other seeds fell on rocky ground, where they had not much soil, and immediately they sprang up, since they had no depth of soil, but when the sun rose they were scorched; and since they had no root they withered away." (vv. 5, 6)

Some people who hear the good news have only a shallow understanding of what it means. So when they meet with temptation or personal hardship or some other difficulty, their faith quickly fades away.

"Other seeds fell upon thorns, and the thorns grew up and choked them." (v. 7)

Some people who hear the good news are distracted by other things. Their attention is taken up with the pursuit of material possessions, or the desire for worldly success, or the pressure of some other concern, and they do not hold to the faith.

"Other seeds fell on good soil and brought forth grain, some a hundredfold, some sixty, some thirty." (v. 8)

But some people who hear the good news develop a deep and single-minded faith that grows to maturity with good works and a pure life.

"He who has ears, let him hear." (v. 9)

Let those sowers, who proclaim the good news, hear and take courage in the face of discouraging results.

May they be renewed in patience and in hope, for God's work will surely find some ready hearts in which to take root and grow.

Let those who hear the good news truly hear and receive the word as the good earth nourishes a seed.

May they long to be rooted and grounded in Christ, undismayed by difficulty and undistracted by the world. Amen.

Meditation/Discussion: Do you identify more closely with Jesus' message to the sower or to the soils? Share a personal experience of proclaiming or receiving God's word. Then pray together for God's continuing work in your lives.

God is Sovereign 23

Introduction: Our sovereign God, almighty, wise, and righteous, we praise you today and as long as we live for your patient and loving reign over all your creatures. Amen.

Reading: (Matthew 13:24–30)

Praise to God almighty, whose dominion and power extends to every corner of the universe.

Praise to God all wise, whose knowledge is unsurpassed and whose ways are beyond understanding.

Praise to God all righteous, whose justice is pure and everlasting.

Yet with our praise, we also bring our questions. If God is everything we proclaim, why then is there still suffering in the world? Why famine and earthquake? Why sickness and disease?

The whole earth labors under the false dominion of the evil one. It waits for the day of liberation when God will set it free from such bondage.

But why is there still injustice in the world? Why poverty? Why cruelty?

Even our own humanity is not untouched by evil. As the earth waits for the day of liberation, we too await the final day of reckoning.

Yet must the wicked prosper as we await this final day? Does God not care that those who work against the kingdom live long and well in the world?

Jesus once told the crowds a parable about this very thing. He began by admitting the presence of both good and evil in the world.

Another parable he put before them, saying, "The kingdom of heaven may be compared to a man who sowed good seed in his field; but while men were sleeping, his enemy came and sowed weeds among the wheat, and went away." (vv. 24, 25)

Jesus even admitted that both good and evil appeared to flourish.

"So when the plants came up and bore grain, then the weeds appeared also. And the servants of the householder came and said to him, 'Sir did you not sow good seed in your field? How then has it weeds?' He said to them, 'An enemy has done this.' " (vv. 26–28a)

But Jesus recognized the importance of timing in the separation of the good from the evil. A householder cannot weed a field without damage to the good grain until harvest. Nor can God root out the wicked without damage to the good, until the day of judgment.

"The servants said to him, 'Then do you want us to go and gather them?' But he said, 'No; lest in gathering the weeds you root up the wheat along with them.' " (vv. 28b, 29)

Judgment belongs to God alone who is patient and slow to anger. But the day is coming when God's justice will fully reign in all the earth.

" 'Let both grow together until the harvest; and at harvest time I will tell the reapers, Gather the weeds first and bind them in bundles to be burned, but gather the wheat into my barn.' " (v. 30)

Prayer: Our gracious God, we're often too quick to condemn and too ready to destroy the things we judge unfit for your kingdom. Teach us to view the world with the same long-suffering patience and love you extend to us. In the name of Jesus, the sower of good seed. Amen.

Have No Fear 24

Introduction: In Jesus Christ, all our fears are laid to rest, for God is present in every time of trial.

Reading: (Matthew 14:22–33)

It's a long way from the first century to the twentieth.

It's a long way from the sea of Galilee to this place of meeting.

Yet in spite of the distance of space and time, we share a common humanity with Jesus' first disciples.

We still know fear in the face of our own mortality. We still need faith to carry us through personal difficulty.

Then Jesus made the disciples get into the boat and go before him to the other side, while he dismissed the crowds. And after he had dismissed the crowds, he went up on the mountain by himself to pray. When evening came, he was there alone, but the boat by this time was many furlongs distant from the land, beaten by the waves; for the wind was against them. (vv. 22–24)

As Jesus' disciples struggled against the waves and wind of the storm, we struggle sometimes against a hostile environment or personal tragedy.

And in the fourth watch of the night he came to them, walking on the sea. (v. 25)

As Jesus came to his disciples even in the midst of the storm, so God comes to us even in the midst of our struggles.

But when the disciples saw him walking on the sea, they were terrified, saying, "It is a ghost!" And they cried out for fear. (v. 26)

As the disciples failed to recognize Jesus walking on the water, sometimes we fail to recognize God's presence in our own lives.

But immediately he spoke to them, saying, "Take heart, it is I; have no fear." (v. 27)

As Jesus assured his disciples of his presence and his power, so God is surely with us and reigns over all.

And Peter answered him, "Lord, if it is you, bid me come to you on the water." He said, "Come." So Peter got out of the boat and walked on the water and came to Jesus; but when he saw the wind, he was afraid, and beginning to sink he cried out, "Lord, save me." (vv. 28–30)

As Peter's fear overwhelmed the strength of his faith, sometimes our fear is more than we can bear.

Jesus immediately reached out his hand and caught him, saying to him, "O man of little faith, why did you doubt?" (v. 31)

Yet as Jesus stood ready to lay hold of Peter, so God stands ready to strengthen us in the time of fear.

And when they got into the boat, the wind ceased. And those in the boat worshiped him, saying, "Truly you are the Son of God." (vv. 32, 33)

As the disciples worshiped Jesus as the Son of God, so do we worship you, our Sovereign God. Amen.

Meditation/Discussion: Think of an instance of fear or struggle in your own life. Did it result in a deeper appreciation of God's presence or power? Why or why not?

Tradition and Truth 25

Introduction: Then said Jesus to the crowds and to his disciples, "The scribes and the Pharisees sit on Moses' seat; so practice and observe whatever they tell you, but not what they do; for they preach, but do not practice." (Matthew 23:1-3)

Reading: (Matthew 15:1-9)

In the law of Moses, God commanded the Hebrew people to distinguish between things clean and unclean.

These were largely ceremonial distinctions, but they were deeply woven into Hebrew life, involving birds and animals, household utensils, houses, land, and even people, under certain circumstances.

By the time of Jesus' earthly ministry, the Pharisees and scribes had expanded these distinctions and their corresponding provisions for cleansing, even beyond what the law of Moses required.

This expanded system was part of their oral commentary on the law, which was known as the tradition of the elders.

Then Pharisees and scribes came to Jesus from Jerusalem and said, "Why do your disciples transgress the tradition of the elders? For they do not wash their hands when they eat." He answered them, "And why do you transgress the commandment of God for the sake of your tradition?" (vv. 1-3)

Jesus answered his questioners with a question of his own. Why did they value their tradition above the law they claimed to follow?

"For God commanded, 'Honor your father and your mother,' and 'He who speaks evil of father or mother, let

him surely die.' But you say, 'If any one tells his father or his mother, What you would have gained from me is given to God, he need not honor his father.' So, for the sake of your tradition you have made void the word of God." (vv. 4-6)

According to the Pharisees and scribes, a person could make a vow consecrating his material possessions to God, and thus be excused from using them to help even his own parents. Instead of supporting the observance of God's law, this tradition of "korban" actually enabled people to break it!

"You hypocrites! Well did Isaiah prophesy of you, when he said: 'This people honors me with their lips, but their heart is far from me; in vain do they worship me, teaching as doctrines the precepts of men.' " (vv. 7-9)

Such hypocrisy is just as unacceptable to God today as it has been at any time in history.

There is more to cleanliness before God than handwashing, for only the pure in heart please God.

There is more to good stewardship than tithing, for all that we have already belongs to God.

There is more to faithful living than regular church attendance, for our walk with God is a daily attendance to justice, mercy, and humility.

There is more to devotional life than daily prayers, for true spirituality is a constant communion with God.

Prayer: O God of all truth, we thank you for the rich heritage of faith that we have received from the past. We know there is much to value in it, yet we realize the need to distinguish between tradition which encourages faithfulness to you and tradition which discourages it. Give us the wisdom to know the difference, we pray. Amen.

Confessing Jesus 26

Introduction: We gather together with a common confession. We confess God our Maker who created us. We confess God the Spirit who brings us together. We confess God our Savior in the person of Jesus Christ.

Reading: (Matthew 16:13–20)

The area of Caesarea Philippi was no stranger to pagan religion. There the ancient Syrians worshiped Baal, and the later Greeks worshiped Pan. There Herod the Great built a temple to the Roman Augustus Caesar.

It was in that setting of the religions of the world that Jesus questioned his disciples about his own identity.

Now when Jesus came into the district of Caesarea Philippi, he asked the disciples, "Who do men say that the Son of man is?" (v. 13)

The crowds, who had heard Jesus teach and had seen him heal the sick and cast out demons, were saying many things about him. And the disciples reported to Jesus the things that they had heard.

And they said, "Some say John the Baptist, others say Elijah, and others Jeremiah or one of the prophets." (v. 14)

But Jesus was not merely interested in popular opinion. He wanted a personal response.

He said to them, "But who do you say that I am?" (v. 15)

As spokesman for the group, it was Simon Peter who answered him.

Simon Peter replied, "You are the Christ, the Son of the living God." (v. 16)

The crowds did not understand who Jesus really was, but Peter's spiritual eyes had been opened.

And Jesus answered him, "Blessed are you, Simon Bar-Jona! For flesh and blood has not revealed this to you, but my Father who is in heaven." (v. 17)

Peter was one of the first to confess Jesus as the Christ, and so he became one of the founding stones of the church.

"And I tell you, you are Peter, and on this rock I will build my church, and the powers of death shall not prevail against it." (v. 18)

As part of Christ's church, Peter had a great responsibility.

"I will give you the keys of the kingdom of heaven, and whatever you bind on earth shall be bound in heaven, and whatever you loose on earth shall be loosed in heaven." (v. 19)

But not everyone was ready to understand Christ and his mission.

Then he strictly charged the disciples to tell no one that he was the Christ. (v. 20)

Today we are faced with the same question: who do we say Jesus is?

And today people give a variety of responses. Some say he was a good man or a prophet or a great teacher.

But we say Jesus was—and is—truly human and truly God.

Prayer: Our God, with Peter, we too are living stones in your church. With Peter we share the same privilege and responsibility of being your church in the world. May we be faithful in this mission you have set before us. In the name of Christ, the chief cornerstone. Amen.

The Transfiguration 27

Introduction: For as the heavens are higher than the earth, so are my ways higher than your ways and my thoughts than your thoughts. (Isaiah 55:9)

Reading: (Matthew 17:1–8)

I don't always understand the way God works in the world. I don't understand natural disasters or personal tragedies, yet I see God bringing wholeness to people in the midst of such situations.

I don't understand broken relationships or armed conflict, yet I see God bringing strength to people even in the moment of crisis.

Sometimes I don't even understand God's leading in my own life, yet as the weeks, months, and years pass by, I see how surely God has led me.

Even Jesus' first disciples didn't always understand the way God worked in the world.

In fact, when Jesus first predicted his coming suffering and death, Peter couldn't accept it as part of Christ's mission. For him, Jesus' death could only mean humiliating defeat.

But Jesus' mission as the suffering Messiah was really part of God's plan of glory. One day God gave a glimpse of this to Peter, James, and John.

And after six days Jesus took with him Peter and James and John his brother, and led them up a high mountain apart. (v. 1)

God confirmed Jesus' mission as the suffering Messiah by a visible display of divine glory.

And he was transfigured before them, and his face shone like the sun, and his garments became white as light. (v. 2)

God confirmed Jesus' mission as the suffering Messiah by the appearance of Moses and Elijah, who affirmed Jesus' fulfillment of both the law and the prophets.

And behold, there appeared to them Moses and Elijah, talking with him. (v. 3)

But Peter did not yet understand what was happening. He was still not ready to see Jesus go on to Jerusalem to certain suffering and death.

And Peter said to Jesus, "Lord, it is well that we are here; if you wish, I will make three booths here, one for you and one for Moses and one for Elijah." (v. 4)

Then God confirmed Jesus' mission as the suffering Messiah by turning Peter's attention back to Jesus.

He was still speaking, when lo, a bright cloud overshadowed them, and a voice from the cloud said, "This is my beloved Son, with whom I am well pleased; listen to him." When the disciples heard this, they fell on their faces, and were filled with awe. But Jesus came and touched them, saying, "Rise, and have no fear." And when they lifted up their eyes, they saw no one but Jesus only. (vv. 5–8)

Still, Peter and the other disciples couldn't fully understand the significance of what they had seen. That would have to wait until Jesus' death and resurrection had actually taken place.

Prayer: Like Jesus' first disciples, sometimes we cannot understand the events of our own lives. But, like them, may we listen to the voice of our God and lift up our eyes to Jesus. Let us rise and have no fear. Amen.

Reconciliation 28

Introduction: Our God, sometimes we fail in our love for a brother or sister. And once we realize a relationship is strained, even then we fail sometimes to make it right again. Help us to care enough about each other to replace our fear, insensitivity, and indifference with true reconciliation. Amen.

Reading: (Matthew 18:15–20)

Wherever people live and work together, there is bound to be the occasional misunderstanding or difference of opinion. There is bound to be some hurt and heartache from the things we say and do. Even among brother and sister in the church we will have our differences.

But more important than our differences is how we handle them. Sometimes we pray about them and hope God will put them to rest. Sometimes we ignore them and hope they will disappear on their own. Sometimes we complain about them to a third party or harbor resentment in our hearts. But there is yet another way.

If your brother sins against you, go and tell him his fault, between you and him alone. If he listens to you, you have gained your brother. (v. 15)

If you feel you have been wronged, do not complain about it to one another or bear a silent grudge against the one who has hurt you. But go to that person with your hurt, and try to resolve it between you.

But if he does not listen, take one or two others along with you, that every word may be confirmed by the evidence of two or three witnesses. (v. 16)

If you cannot resolve your differences alone, ask one or two other people for assistance. A third party not directly involved in your situation may bring a fresh perspective to your relationship.

If he refuses to listen to them, tell it to the church. (v. 17a)

If you are still unable to resolve your differences, take it to the church for additional counsel and guidance. But if even the church's efforts do not result in reconciliation, further direct action to mend your relationship is impossible.

And if he refuses to listen even to the church, let him be to you as a Gentile and a tax collector. (v. 17b)

By refusing to accept counsel, the one who has wronged you has severed your fellowship. Yet you are called to continue your love for that person even as Jesus loved the Gentile and the tax collector.

Truly, I say to you, whatever you bind on earth shall be bound in heaven, and whatever you loose on earth shall be loosed in heaven. Again I say to you, if two of you agree on earth about anything they ask, it will be done for them by my Father in heaven. For where two or three are gathered in my name, there am I in the midst of them. (vv. 18–20)

As members of the church we are responsible to seek reconciliation together with one another. And Jesus himself has promised to be with us as we attempt to work out our differences as his disciples.

We may not always be able to bring complete healing to every relationship.

Yet together in the church we can face the pain of being human.

Meditation/Discussion: What would it mean for you to love someone the way Jesus loved Gentiles and tax collectors?

Forgiving One Another 29

Introduction: Our merciful God, we know you have forgiven us so often and for so many things. We ask for your help in being as generous with each other as you have been with us. Amen.

Reading: (Matthew 18:23-34)

Therefore the kingdom of heaven may be compared to a king who wished to settle accounts with his servants. When he began the reckoning, one was brought to him who owed him ten thousand talents; and as he could not pay, his lord ordered him to be sold, with his wife and children and all that he had, and payment to be made. (vv. 23-25)

But to avoid slavery for himself and his family, the servant begged his master for mercy.

So the servant fell on his knees, imploring him, "Lord, have patience with me, and I will pay you everything." (v. 26)

But the lord knew that the servant could never repay the debt, for such a large sum was more than a person could earn in an entire lifetime. It was even more than the servant and his family could gain by going into slavery.

And out of pity for him the lord of that servant released him and forgave him the debt. (v. 27)

But the servant quickly forgot the compassion of his lord. He had hardly left his master's presence before he began to abuse one of his coworkers who owed him a small sum of money.

But that same servant, as he went out, came upon one of his fellow servants who owed him a hundred denarii; and seizing him by the throat he said, "Pay what you owe." So his fellow servant fell down and besought him, "Have patience with me, and I will pay you." He refused and went and put him in prison till he should pay the debt. (vv. 28–30)

In spite of the small amount of this debt compared to his own, the forgiven servant would not forgive his debtor. He would not even agree to wait for his payment.

When his fellow servants saw what had taken place, they were greatly distressed, and they went and reported to their lord all that had taken place. (v. 31)

When the lord heard their reports, he was angry at the first servant's hardness of heart, and he would not tolerate such lack of compassion.

Then his lord summoned him and said to him, "You wicked servant! I forgave you all that debt because you besought me; and should not you have had mercy on your fellow servant, as I had mercy on you?" And in anger his lord delivered him to the jailers, till he should pay all his debt. (vv. 32–34)

Our God, help us to hear the truth of this parable in our own lives.

We are servants of God and coworkers with one another.

Our God, help us to see the truth of this parable in our own lives.

God has patience with us, and so we need to have patience with one another.

Our God, help us to live the truth of this parable in our own lives.

God has forgiven us, and so we need to forgive one another. Amen.

Meditation/Discussion: How does our refusal to forgive someone damage our relationship with God and with other people?

Partnership with God 30

Introduction: Our God, today we thank you for this time we can spend together as partners in worship. May we continue to grow in friendship and in mutual love for you. Amen.

Reading: (Matthew 19:3–12)

We were created for partnership with God.

We were created for partnership with one another.

Together we have communion with God.

Together we work to further God's reign of peace and justice in the world.

We are partners in the church, when we worship and work together as the communion of saints.

We are partners in the family, when we grow together as a body of mutual nurture.

Some of us are partners in marriage, when we commit ourselves to live together as a new creation.

One day some Pharisees asked Jesus a question about the nature of marriage.

And Pharisees came up to him and tested him by asking, "Is it lawful to divorce one's wife for any cause?" He answered, "Have you not read that he who made them from the beginning made them male and female, and said, 'For this reason a man shall leave his father and mother and be joined to his wife, and the two shall become one flesh'? So they are no longer two but one flesh. What therefore God has joined together, let not man put asunder." (vv. 3–6)

Marriage is a wholehearted commitment. It is a union meant to last.

They said to him, "Why then did Moses command one to give a certificate of divorce, and to put her away?" He said to them, "For your hardness of heart Moses allowed you to divorce your wives, but from the beginning it was not so. And I say to you: whoever divorces his wife, except for unchastity, and marries another, commits adultery." (vv. 7–9)

Marriage is not for everyone. Only those to whom God has given the gift of marriage can live in such a committed relationship.

The disciples said to him, "If such is the case of a man with his wife, it is not expedient to marry." But he said to them, "Not all men can receive this saying, but only those to whom it is given. For there are eunuchs who have been so from birth, and there are eunuchs who have been made eunuchs by men, and there are eunuchs who have made themselves eunuchs for the sake of the kingdom of heaven. He who is able to receive this, let him receive it." (vv. 10–12)

God does not call every one of us to partnership in marriage.

But God calls every one of us to partnership in the new community of the church.

God does not call every one of us to remain single for the sake of the work of God.

But whatever our station in life, God calls every one of us to work for peace and justice there.

Prayer: O God, giver of every good thing, we thank you for the many opportunities for partnership in the church, our families, and friendships. Thank you particularly for the gifts of singlehood and marriage. Whichever gift you grant us, may we receive it with joy and live it to the fullest in your love and service. Amen.

Eternity in Our Hearts 31

Introduction: For everything there is a season, and a time for every matter under heaven . . . . (Ecclesiastes 3:1)

Reading: (Matthew 19:13–15)

When I was a child, some days time almost seemed to stand still for me. It took too long to wait for tomorrow and forever for summer to come.

It was a long time between birthdays, and being grown up was just a distant dream.

Now time trickles through my fingers and is gone all too fast.

There never seems to be enough time for everything I need and want to do.

Time waits for no one.

So we scramble to keep up with it.

Time flies.

So we fly from home to work to church and back again.

We are always in a hurry, and we don't like interruptions.

Yet Jesus did not prevent people from interrupting him. Even on his way to raise a ruler's daughter from the dead, he stopped to speak to a woman in need of healing.

Even near the end of his earthly ministry, as he traveled to Jerusalem and to the cross, he stopped to bless some children.

Then children were brought to him that he might lay his hands on them and pray. (v. 13a)

Jesus' disciples wanted to spare him from what they saw as an unnecessary interruption. They thought he didn't have enough time to spend with these children.

The disciples rebuked the people; but Jesus said, "Let the children come to me, and do not hinder them; for to such belongs the kingdom of heaven." (vv. 13b, 14)

Jesus did not treat the children as an interruption. They too had a place in God's loving care.

And he laid his hands on them and went away. (v. 15)

For Jesus, there was time for children even as he journeyed to the cross.

There was time for men and for women, for Jews and for Gentiles, for rich and for poor.

There was time for the sick, for the persons with disabilities, and even for the dead.

For us too there is time, for God has created us for eternity.

There is time for children, for they are the ones God has given to us to nurture.

There is time to talk with people in need, for they are the people God has given us to love.

There is time for interruptions, for they are the opportunities God has given us for service.

So set eternity in our hearts, O God, and we will keep your time. Amen.

Meditation/Discussion: How do you respond to interruptions in your own lives? Are they blessings or bothers? Why?

The Rich in This World 32

Introduction: As for the rich in this world, charge them not to be haughty, nor to set their hopes on uncertain riches but on God who richly furnishes us with everything to enjoy. (1 Timothy 6:17)

Reading: (Matthew 19:16–22)

We are the rich in this world.

We rely on our money and our material possessions to see us through our lives.

We get caught up in the pursuit of more and better material goods.

We define people by their occupation and level of income.

And in our preoccupation with earthly things, we lose sight of their dangers.

Riches encourage pride and a false independence. One young man even thought that he might gain eternal life by his own efforts, but Jesus pointed him to God.

And behold, one came up to him, saying, "Teacher, what good deed must I do, to have eternal life?" And he said to him, "Why do you ask me about what is good? One there is who is good. If you would enter life, keep the commandments." (vv. 16, 17)

Riches tend to make us selfish. Perhaps this young man had neglected to love and serve other people, for Jesus pointed him to the commandments dealing with personal relationships.

He said to him, "Which?" And Jesus said, "You shall not kill, You shall not commit adultery, You shall not steal, You shall not bear false witness, Honor your father and mother, and You shall love your neighbor as yourself." (vv. 18, 19)

Riches are not ultimately satisfying. In spite of the young man's possessions and in spite of his efforts to keep the law, he knew there was something missing from his life.

The young man said to him, "All these I have observed; what do I still lack?" Jesus said to him, "If you would be perfect, go sell what you possess and give it to the poor, and you will have treasure in heaven; and come, follow me." (vv. 20, 21)

Riches can keep us from following Christ. This young man could not let go of his possessions even to gain the eternal life which he sought.

When the young man heard this he went away sorrowful; for he had great possessions. (v. 22)

It is hard for a rich person to acknowledge the reign of God, for riches encourage pride, a false independence, and a selfish spirit.

It is hard for us to acknowledge the reign of God, for we are the rich of this world. We tend to get carried away by our own pride, independence, and self-centeredness.

O God, take our pride from us, and teach us to see ourselves as we really are.

O God, take our false independence from us, and teach us to rely on you.

O God, take our self-centeredness from us, and teach us to follow you.

We ask these things through Jesus Christ, for with God nothing is impossible. Amen.

Meditation/Discussion: Have you ever thought of yourselves as "the rich in this world" like this young man? Why or why not?

The Way of Servanthood 33

Introduction: We gather together as servants of God and servants of one another. We gather together in the name of God's great Servant, Jesus Christ. Amen.

Reading: (Matthew 20:20–28)

Sometimes the kingdom of God seems like a kingdom of contradictions.

In losing our lives for Christ's sake, we live.

In giving ourselves in service, we receive.

In weakness, we find strength.

Even the idea of what it means to be great is completely turned around.

If we want to be great in the kingdom of God, we must acknowledge our dependence on God.

Then the mother of the sons of Zebedee came up to Jesus, with her sons, and kneeling before him she asked him for something. And he said to her, "What do you want?" She said to him, "Command that these two sons of mine may sit, one at your right hand and one at your left, in your kingdom." (vv. 20, 21)

If we want to be great in the kingdom of God, we must follow Jesus in sacrifice and suffering.

But Jesus answered, "You do not know what you are asking. Are you able to drink the cup that I am to drink?" They said to him, "We are able." (v. 22)

If we want to be great in the kingdom of God, we must leave our future in the hands of God.

He said to them, "You will drink my cup, but to sit at my right hand and at my left is not mine to grant, but it is for those for whom it has been prepared by my Father." (v. 23)

If we want to be great in the kingdom of God, we must not seek honor and authority, for selfish ambition leads to jealousy and strife.

And when the ten heard it, they were indignant at the two brothers (v. 24)

If we want to be great in the kingdom of God, we must follow Jesus in pouring out our lives in service to God and to other people.

But Jesus called them to him and said, "You know that the rulers of the Gentiles lord it over them, and their great men exercise authority over them. It shall not be so among you: but whoever would be great among you must be your servant, and whoever would be first among you must be your slave; even as the Son of man came not to be served but to serve, and to give his life as a ransom for many." (vv. 25–28)

In the kingdom of God, leadership is servanthood, for Jesus himself led the way in service.

Our God, teach us to care for the needs of the people in your world. Like Jesus, may we find greatness in servanthood and lead others to you by our service.

In the kingdom of God, glory is found in sacrifice, for Jesus himself was glorified in his death and resurrection.

Our God, teach us to sacrifice our own narrow definitions of success. Like Jesus, may we be content with the work of service that you have given us and know the reward of serving you. Amen.

Meditation/Discussion: What work of service has God given you as individuals or as a team? What sacrifices has it required of you?

An Acted Parable 34

Introduction: This was to fulfill what was spoken by the prophet: "I will open my mouth in parables, I will utter what has been hidden since the foundation of the world." (Matthew 13:35)

Reading: (Matthew 21:1–11)

Jesus' teaching was full of parables.

When he talked about the work of God, he told of a sower scattering seed and a woman baking bread.

When he talked about God's love for people, he told of a woman searching for her lost coin and a father waiting for his prodigal son.

When he talked about prayer, he told of a friend in need of food and a woman before an unjust judge.

And so when Jesus prepared to enter Jerusalem for the last time, he chose yet another parable. But this time it was a parable without words, for the story unfolded right before the people's eyes.

And when they drew near to Jerusalem and came to Bethphage, to the Mount of Olives, then Jesus sent two disciples, saying to them, "Go into the village opposite you, and immediately you will find an ass tied, and a colt with her; untie them and bring them to me. If any one says anything to you, you shall say, 'The Lord has need of them,' and he will send them immediately." (vv. 1–3)

Jesus planned to display his identity as the Messiah more openly than ever before, just as the prophet Zechariah had predicted.

This took place to fulfill what was spoken by the prophet, saying, "Tell the daughter of Zion, Behold, your king is coming to you, humble, and mounted on an ass, and on a colt, the foal of an ass." (vv. 4, 5)

When everything was ready, Jesus rode into the city boldly. Even though he knew the authorities opposed him, the signs of victory were everywhere in the palm branches carried by the crowds.

The disciples went and did as Jesus had directed them; they brought the ass and the colt, and put their garments on them, and he sat thereon. Most of the crowd spread their garments on the road, the others cut branches from the trees and spread them on the road. (vv. 6-8)

The crowds were in the mood for celebration, and they greeted Jesus with cries of blessing and thanksgiving to God.

And the crowds that went before him and that followed him shouted, "Hosanna to the Son of David! Blessed is he who comes in the name of the Lord! Hosanna in the highest!" (v. 9)

And yet, like all of Jesus' stories and miracles, this acted parable was also subject to misunderstanding.

And when he entered Jerusalem, all the city was stirred, saying, "Who is this?" And the crowds said, "This is the prophet Jesus from Nazareth of Galilee." (vv. 10, 11)

Once again, the majority of the people saw only a prophet. They failed to recognize Jesus as the Messiah who fulfilled the Scriptures.

"Who is this?" the crowds asked.

This is Jesus Christ, truly human and truly God.

Prayer: Our God, we thank you for your persistence in communicating your loving purposes to the world. Thank you for never giving up on us. Amen.

God's Great Promise 35

Introduction: Praise to our God who has promised to be with us at all times. Praise to our God who fulfills every promise in the person of Jesus Christ. Amen.

Reading: (Matthew 21:12–16)

From Genesis to Malachi, God's greatest promise to the people of Israel was the promise of a Messiah.

The prophet Malachi wrote of Christ's coming. He said, "The Lord whom you seek will suddenly come to his temple." (Malachi 3:1)

And Jesus entered the temple of God and drove out all who sold and bought in the temple, and he overturned the tables of the moneychangers and the seats of those who sold pigeons. (v. 12)

The prophet Jeremiah wrote of Christ's temple. He said, "Has this house, which is called by my name, become a den of robbers in your eyes? Behold, I myself have seen it, says the Lord." (Jeremiah 7:11)

He said to them, "It is written, 'My house shall be called a house of prayer': but you make it a den of robbers." (v. 13)

The prophet Isaiah wrote of Christ's day. He said, "Then the eyes of the blind shall be opened, and the ears of the deaf unstopped; then shall the lame man leap like a hart, and the tongue of the dumb sing for joy." (Isaiah 35:5, 6a)

And the blind and the lame came to him in the temple, and he healed them. (v. 14)

The psalmist wrote of Christ's earthly opponents. He said, "The kings of the earth set themselves, and the rulers take counsel together, against the lord and his anointed." (Psalm 2:2)

But when the chief priests and the scribes saw the wonderful things that he did, and the children crying out in the temple, "Hosanna to the Son of David!" they were indignant; and they said to him, "Do you hear what these are saying?" (vv. 15, 16a)

The psalmist also wrote of Christ's glory. He said, "O Lord, our Lord, how majestic is thy name in all the earth! Thou whose glory above the heavens is chanted by the mouth of babes and infants." (Psalms 8:1, 2)

And Jesus said to them, "Yes; have you never read, 'Out of the mouth of babes and sucklings thou has brought perfect praise'?" (v. 16b)

Jesus entered the temple as the promised Messiah of God.

We wait for the promised return of the resurrected and glorified Christ.

Jesus renewed the temple as a house of prayer.

We wait for the promised renewal of heaven and earth as the sanctuary of God.

Jesus renewed the temple as a house of healing.

We wait for the promised healing of all our afflictions.

Jesus renewed the temple as a house of praise.

We wait for the promised day when every voice will join with us in praise to God.

Praise to our God!

Meditation/Discussion: Where have you seen the fulfillment of God's promises in your own life? Give thanks to God for them as you pray together.

The True Vineyard 36

Introduction: Thou didst bring a vine out of Egypt; thou didst drive out the nations and plant it. Thou didst clear the ground for it; it took deep root and filled the land. (Psalm 80:8, 9)

Reading: (Matthew 21:33–41)

Hear another parable. There was a householder who planted a vineyard, and set a hedge around it, and dug a wine press in it, and built a tower, and let it out to tenants, and went into another country. (v. 33)

God is the householder who planted the people of Israel in the promised land as a good vineyard. God protected them from their enemies, provided for their needs, and charged their leaders to care for them.

When the season of fruit drew near, he sent his servants to the tenants, to get his fruit; and the tenants took his servants and beat one, killed another, and stoned another. (vv. 34, 35)

In the course of time, God sent the prophets, but they were rejected by the very ones God had chosen to lead the people.

Again he sent other servants, more than the first; and they did the same to them. (v. 36)

Still God was patient and sent more prophets. But these too were treated as false prophets.

Afterward he sent his son to them, saying, "They will respect my son." But when the tenants saw the son, they said to themselves, "This is the heir; come, let us kill him and have his inheritance." And they took him and cast him out of the vineyard, and killed him. (vv. 37-39)

Finally God came to speak to the people in the person of Jesus Christ. But they treated Jesus no better than the prophets before him, and they crucified him as an outcast.

When therefore the owner of the vineyard comes, what will he do to those tenants? They said to him, "He will put those wretches to a miserable death, and let out the vineyard to other tenants who will give him the fruits in their seasons." (vv. 40, 41)

Therefore, God has chosen a new people of repentance, faith, and obedience to bear the fruit of God's household.

We are the new people of God through repentance from our own way of life.

Help us, O God, to turn to you and receive the new and fruitful life you offer to all your followers.

We are the new people of God through faith in Jesus Christ.

Help us, O God, to accept the reign of Christ and live as he did in faithful relationship with you and with other people.

We are the new people of God through obedience to God's word.

Help us, O God, to do your will with ready, thankful hearts.

We are the new people of God through God's mercy in Jesus Christ.

Help us, O God, to be a true vineyard bearing fruit to the glory of your name. Amen.

Meditation/Discussion: What kind of good fruit do you think God expects from you? How can you help each other to cultivate these qualities or activities in your own lives?

In the Image of God 37

Introduction: Our God, we thank you for the great privilege of bearing your image. We ask you to make us worthy of this task, that we may truly reflect the glory and holiness that is yours. In the name of Jesus, who showed us your character most clearly. Amen.

Reading: (Matthew 22:15–22)

The Jewish authorities often came into conflict with Jesus' way of life.

They resented his disregard for their tradition.

They criticized his association with sinners.

They questioned his teaching.

Yet Jesus was unafraid to confront them.

Sometimes he spoke out against their hypocrisy, but he never stooped to petty or unfair criticism.

Sometimes he expressed his anger at their lack of love, but he never lost his self-control.

Sometimes he wept over their stubbornness, but he never failed to show God's way to them.

Then the Pharisees went and took counsel how to entangle him in his talk. And they sent their disciples to him, along with the Herodians, saying, "Teacher, we know that you are true, and teach the way of God truthfully, and care for no man; for you do not regard the position of men. Tell us, then, what you think. Is it lawful to pay taxes to Caesar, or not?" (vv. 15–17)

But the Pharisees and the Herodians could not deceive Jesus with their flattery. He knew they were more interested in damaging his reputation than in hearing God's word.

But Jesus, aware of their malice, said, "Why put me to the test, you hypocrites? Show me the money for the tax." And they brought him a coin. (vv. 18, 19)

Jesus gave them a carefully worded answer which avoided their trap and provided sound teaching as well.

And Jesus said to them, "Whose likeness and inscription is this?" They said, "Ceasar's." Then he said to them, "Render therefore to Caesar the things that are Caesar's, and to God the things that are God's." (vv. 20, 21)

Jesus' opponents failed in their attempt to discredit him, for they could find no fault with his saying.

When they heard it, they marvelled; and they left him and went away. (v. 22)

Jesus managed to avoid the trap of the Pharisees and the Herodians.

He also set down a principle of kingdom living for his followers.

Give to Caesar the things that are Caesar's.

Give to God the things that are God's.

But what belongs to Caesar?

What belongs to God?

The coin for the tax bore the image of Caesar. It belonged to the Roman government authorities.

We bear the image of God. We belong to the kingdom of heaven.

Meditation/Discussion: Where can you see the image of God in yourself? In one another? What difference does this make in the way you live?

The Great Commandment 38

Introduction: Our God, we thank you for the many things you have taught us through the Scriptures, through the example of your life in Jesus Christ, through the people and circumstances of our own lives, through the Spirit you sent to be our guide. Forgive us where we have rejected your teaching, rekindle our willingness to learn from you. Amen.

Reading: (Matthew 22:34–40)

During his early ministry, Jesus often met with opposition to his teaching.

It must have been tempting to give up hope for a people so stubborn and self-righteous.

Even within his own circle of disciples, Jesus regularly confronted lack of belief and misunderstanding.

It must have been tempting to abandon the task of teaching a people so slow to faith.

Yet even more grievous then the people's stubbornness and the disciples' misunderstandings, were the deliberate attempts by the Jewish establishment to undermine Jesus' reputation.

Time after time, the Sadducees, Pharisees, and scribes tried to provoke Jesus into saying or doing something contrary to the law or unpopular with the crowds.

Yet time after time, Jesus handled their questions and accusations in a manner above reproach by opponents and public alike.

But when the Pharisees heard that he had silenced the Sadducees, they came together. And one of them, a lawyer, asked him a question, to test him. "Teacher, which is the great commandment in the law?" (vv. 34–36)

Jesus directed him back to the book of Deuteronomy for guidance.

And he said to him, "You shall love the Lord your God with all your heart, and with all your soul, and with all your mind. This is the great and first commandment." (vv. 37, 38)

But Jesus did not stop there. He linked this commandment with another one from the book of Leviticus.

"And a second is like it, You shall love your neighbor as yourself." (v. 39)

With these two great commandments, Jesus declared the essence of God's will.

"On these two commandments depend all the law and the prophets." (v. 40)

Once again, the Pharisees could find no fault with Jesus' teaching.

Once again, Jesus gave good instruction and managed to avoid their trap as well.

Our God, teach us to accept the authority of this instruction for our own lives.

Love your God with all your heart, soul, and mind, with everything you have and everything you are.

Our God, teach us to love you wholeheartedly in sincere and active service.

Love your neighbor as yourself, with a lasting patience and kind regard.

Our God, teach us to love our neighbors freely in both word and deed. Amen.

Meditation/Discussion: What is the relationship between loving God and loving your neighbor? How does that work out in practice?

Scribes and Pharisees 39

Introduction: Woe to you, scribes and Pharisees, hypocrites! (Matthew 23:23a)

Reading: (Matthew 23:37–39)

Why did Jesus criticize the scribes and the Pharisees so harshly? Did they not preach God's law?

They preached God's law, but they did not practice it.

Did they not wear their phylacteries as God commanded them through Moses?

They practiced the letter of the law, but they neglected its central intent of love for God and for other people.

Did they not travel far and wide in search of converts?

They found their converts, but they made them just as hypocritical as they themselves were.

Did they not tithe everything they had, even the smallest of herbs?

They practiced the tithe, but they neglected justice, mercy, and faith.

Yet for all their faults, Jesus still longed to gather them close to God.

O Jerusalem, Jerusalem, killing the prophets and stoning those who are sent to you! How often would I have gathered your children together as a hen gathers her brood under her wings, and you would not! (v. 37)

But because they rejected him, Christ could not save them from destruction.

Behold, your house is forsaken and desolate. For I tell you, you will not see me again, until you say, "Blessed is he who comes in the name of the Lord." (vv. 38, 39)

Jesus' words were soon to be fulfilled. By A.D. 70 the temple lay in ruins at the hands of the Romans. Today there is still no temple.

Today, Jesus still longs to gather people close to God, if we are willing.

But does our own hypocrisy prevent us from receiving the fullness of Christ's blessing?

Forgive us, our God, when we do not practice the principles we claim to believe. May we be obedient to you in both word and deed.

Does our own practice of religious traditions keep us from loving God and loving other people?

Forgive us, our God, when we equate our own customs with true religion. May we learn to focus ourselves on you alone.

Does our own desire to spread the gospel hinder others from coming to faith in God?

Forgive us, our God, when we count souls instead of caring for people. May we reach out to others in love and personal commitment.

Does our own preoccupation with religious details distract us from practicing justice, mercy, and faith?

Forgive us, our God, when we pride ourselves on our donations to charity and yet deny justice to the poor and the powerless. May we learn to practice justice, mercy, and faithfulness in our daily lives. Amen.

Meditation/Discussion: Choose one of the four questions raised in the last section of the reading for your own reflection.

Until Christ Comes 40

Introduction: Our God, we know you are present with us here, and yet we also know that you will return again in Jesus Christ. We wait in expectation of that final day of salvation.

Reading: (Matthew 24:42-51)

We cannot see the future.

But we walk by faith, not sight.

We cannot number the years of our lives.

But we trust them to the hands of God.

We cannot know the day and hour of the coming of the Lord.

But we know that Christ will come again in glory.

Watch therefore, for you do not know on what day your Lord is coming. (v. 42)

Some of us watch for signs of Christ's return. We look at our world situation for clues that the end is near.

But know this, that if the householder had known in what part of the night the thief was coming, he would have watched and would not have let his house be broken into. (v. 43)

As the householder could not have known when the thief would come, so we cannot know when Christ will return.

Therefore you also must be ready; for the Son of man is coming at an hour you do not expect. (v. 44)

So let us live in expectation of Christ's coming in obedience to God's word.

Who then is the faithful and wise servant, whom his master has set over his household, to give them their food at the proper time? (v. 45)

We are the servants of God, set in the world to do God's work at the appointed time.

Blessed is that servant whom his master when he comes will find so doing. Truly, I say to you, he will set him over all his possessions. (vv. 46, 47)

The faithful servant does the master's work and welcomes him with joy when he comes.

But if that wicked servant says to himself, "My master is delayed," and begins to beat his fellow servants, and eats and drinks with the drunken, the master of that servant will come on a day when he does not expect him and at an hour he does not know, and will punish him, and put him with the hypocrites; there men will weep and gnash their teeth. (vv. 48–51)

The unfaithful servant neglects the master's work and faces judgment.

May we be your faithful servants, O God.

Grant us patience for your coming, that we may not fall into idleness, carelessness, or disobedience.

May we be your wise servants, O God.

Grant us hope for your coming, that we may continue to pray, plan, and work for God's glory in anticipation of Christ's return. Amen.

Meditation/Discussion: What work has God entrusted to you as individuals or as a team? What specific steps are you taking to accomplish it? You may find it helpful to write these down and review them from time to time.

Servants of Joy 41

Introduction: We praise our Creator who has made us with many gifts and abilities. May we learn to use them wisely in tending God's good creation. Amen.

Reading: (Matthew 25:14–28)

For it will be as when a man going on a journey called his servants and entrusted to them his property; to one he gave five talents, to another two, to another one, to each according to his ability. Then he went away. (vv. 14, 15)

To each of us, God has granted a variety of natural abilities and spiritual gifts. God has also given us family, friends, and the support of the Christian community.

He who had received the five talents went at once and traded with them; and he made five talents more. So also, he who had the two talents made two talents more. But he who had received the one talent went and dug in the ground and hid his master's money. (vv. 16–18)

Some of us exercise our abilities. We participate in the lives of the people God has brought our way. But some of us take no part or delight in these things. Through preoccupation with our own desires, through fear of failure, through laziness, we neglect our responsibilities.

Now after a long time the master of those servants came and settled accounts with them. And he who had received the five talents came forward, bringing five talents more, saying, "Master, you delivered to me five talents; here I have made five talents more." His master said to him, "Well done, good and faithful servant; you have been faithful over a little, I will set you over much; enter into the joy of your master." And he also who had the two talents came forward, saying, "Master, you delivered to me two talents;

here I have made two talents more." His master said to him, "Well done, good and faithful servant; you have been faithful over a little, I will set you over much; enter into the joy of your master." (vv. 19–23)

Those that take an active responsibility for their gifts find that their gifts grow and develop. They experience God's own joy and receive even greater opportunities for service and blessing.

He also who had received the one talent came forward, saying, "Master, I knew you to be a hard man, reaping where you did not sow, and gathering where you did not winnow; so I was afraid, and I went and hid your talent in the ground. Here you have what is yours." But his master answered him, "You wicked and slothful servant! You knew that I reap where I have not sowed, and gather where I have not winnowed? Then you ought to have invested my money with the bankers, and at my coming I should have received what was my own with interest. So take the talent from him, and give it to him who has the ten talents." (vv. 24–28)

But those who do not live responsibly with what they have, experience no increase. They are excluded from God's own joy.

So let us set aside our preoccupation with other things, our fear of failure, and our spirit of laziness.

Let us work with the gifts that God has chosen to give us, no matter how few or how humble we may think them.

Prayer: Let us take the responsibility and the risk of living for Christ, and let us enter into God's own joy. Amen.

The Work of Faith 42

Introduction: If a brother or sister is ill-clad and in lack of daily food, and one of you says to them, "Go in peace, be warmed and filled," without giving them the things needed for the body, what does it profit? (James 2:15, 16)

Reading: (Matthew 25:31–45)

When the Son of man comes in his glory, and all the angels with him, then he will sit on his glorious throne. Before him will be gathered all the nations, and he will separate them one from another as a shepherd separates the sheep from the goats, and he will place the sheep at his right hand, but the goats at the left. (vv. 31–33)

In that day, God will judge the nations for their faith and their works, for true faith is active in practical service to others. It does not stop at a heartfelt prayer or a spoken blessing.

Then the King will say to those at his right hand, "Come, O blessed of my Father, inherit the kingdom prepared for you from the foundation of the world; for I was hungry and you gave me food, I was thirsty and you gave me drink, I was a stranger and you welcomed me, I was naked and you clothed me, I was sick and you visited me, I was in prison and you came to me." (vv. 34–36)

The work of faith does not always require a great sum of money or even a special ability. It can be as simple as a cup of water or a visit for the afternoon.

Then the righteous will answer him, "Lord, when did we see thee hungry and feed thee, or thirsty and give thee drink? And when did we see thee a stranger and welcome thee, or naked and clothe thee? And when did we see thee sick or in prison and visit thee?" (vv. 37–39)

The work of faith is unself-conscious. It does not look for the profit of earth or the reward of heaven.

And the King will answer them, "Truly, I say to you, as you did it to one of the least of these my brethren, you did it to me." (v. 40)

The work of faith receives God's blessing. It is cause for rejoicing with God, for by serving the poor, the stranger, and the imprisoned, we serve Christ.

Then he will say to those at his left hand, "Depart from me, you cursed, into the eternal fire prepared for the devil and his angels; for I was hungry and you gave me no food, I was thirsty and you gave me no drink, I was a stranger and you did not welcome me, naked and you did not clothe me, sick and in prison and you did not visit me." (vv. 41–43)

The failure to serve others receives God's judgment. It is cause for separation from God, for by refusing to serve the poor, the stranger, and the imprisoned, we refuse to serve Christ.

Then they also will answer, "Lord, when did we see thee hungry or thirsty or a stranger or naked or sick or in prison, and did not minister to thee?" Then he will answer them, "Truly, I say to you, as you did it not to one of the least of these, you did it not to me." (vv. 44, 45)

Prayer: Our most holy God, this parable of judgment is a hard one for us to hear. But as we reflect on it, may we grow in our understanding of the relationship between faith in you and service to others. May we learn to minister in your name, not from fear of future judgment, but as a genuine response to the love you first gave us. Amen.

Remembering Our God 43

Introduction: Then take heed lest you forget the Lord who brought you out of the land of Egypt, out of the house of bondage. (Deuteronomy 6:12)

Reading: (Matthew 26:26–32)

How could the Israelites have forgotten the God who performed so many wonders to bring them out of Egypt?

How can we forget the God who raised Christ from the dead to bring us out of bondage to sin and death?

At times the Israelites lived as if God had not delivered them.

At times we live as if Christ has not delivered us.

At times the Israelites turned away from God to follow pagan idols.

At times we turn away from God to follow our own desires.

Like the Israelites, we tend to be forgetful people. We're easily distracted from the faith.

Like the Israelites, we need to be reminded of God's work in history. We need to be reminded of God's work even in our own lives today.

Now as they were eating, Jesus took bread, and blessed, and broke it, and gave it to the disciples and said, "Take, eat; this is my body." (v. 26)

With the bread, O God, we remember Christ's body, broken for us in suffering on the cross.

And he took a cup, and when he had given thanks he gave it to them, saying, "Drink of it, all of you; for this is my blood of the covenant, which is poured out for many for the forgiveness of sins." (vv. 27, 28)

With the cup, O God, we remember Christ's blood, shed for us in his death on the cross.

"I tell you I shall not drink again of this fruit of the vine until that day when I drink it new with you in my Father's kingdom." (v. 29)

With these words, O God, we remember Christ's coming again in glory.

And when they had sung a hymn, they went out to the Mount of Olives. Then Jesus said to them, "You will all fall away because of me this night; for it is written, 'I will strike the shepherd, and the sheep of the flock will be scattered.' " (vv. 30, 31)

With these words, O God, we remember Christ's life as the good Shepherd, the one who leads us to you even today.

"But after I am raised up, I will go before you to Galilee." (v. 32)

With these words, O God, we remember Christ's resurrection in victory over sin and death.

Each time we take bread or drink, each time we hear God's Word, may we remember the life, death, and resurrection of Jesus Christ.

Each time we take bread or drink, each time we hear God's Word, may we renew our commitment to follow Christ.

Prayer: Thank you, God, for leaving us with such a gracious reminder of Christ's sacrifice. May we celebrate our new life with you and with your people whenever we take bread or drink—at special times of church communion, but also around the family dinner table, or sharing a meal with friends. Amen.

Companions on the Way 44

Introduction: Our God, we thank you for each other, for families, friends, and coworkers, for the people we meet each day. Amen.

Reading: (Matthew 26:36–46)

We need each other for human companionship.

God said that it is not good for a person to be alone.

We need each other to give and to receive love and encouragement.

God calls us to share one another's joys and to bear one another's burdens.

Even Jesus needed the companionship of others.

During the years of his public ministry, he chose twelve disciples to be with him almost constantly.

Then Jesus went with them to a place called Gethsemane, and he said to his disciples, "Sit here, while I go yonder and pray." (v. 36)

He chose Peter, James, and John to be with him even more intimately.

And taking with him Peter and the two sons of Zebedee, he began to be sorrowful and troubled. (v. 37)

Jesus needed his disciples to wait with him.

Then he said to them, "My soul is very sorrowful, even to death; remain here, and watch with me." And going a little farther he fell on his face and prayed, "My Father, if it be possible, let this cup pass from me; nevertheless, not as I will, but as thou wilt." (vv. 38, 39)

But the disciples failed even to stay awake.

And he came to the disciples and found them sleeping; and he said to Peter, "So, could you not watch with me one hour? Watch and pray that you may not enter into temptation; the spirit indeed is willing, but the flesh is weak." Again, for the second time, he went away and prayed, "My Father, if this cannot pass unless I drink it, thy will be done." (vv. 40–42)

Yet in spite of Jesus' personal agony, the disciples still could not wait with him.

And again he came and found them sleeping, for their eyes were heavy. So, leaving them again, he went away and prayed for the third time, saying the same words. (vv. 43, 44)

Though the disciples failed him, God did not. Through prayer Jesus received such conviction and strength that he was prepared to meet his betrayer and to face the ordeal of false accusation and execution.

Then he came to the disciples and said to them, "Are you still sleeping and taking your rest? Behold, the hour is at hand, and the Son of man is betrayed into the hands of sinners. Rise, let us be going; see, my betrayer is at hand." (vv. 45, 46)

Jesus needed his disciples, but they failed to stand with him in the hour of crisis.

We need each other, but we know there will be times when we feel we stand alone.

Yet even then God will be with us.

Meditation/Discussion: How did Jesus react to the disciples when he found them sleeping? What can we learn from his example for our own response when other people fail us?

The Will of God 45

Introduction: Do not be conformed to this world but be transformed by the renewal of your mind, that you may prove what is the will of God, what is good and acceptable and perfect. (Romans 12:2)

Reading: (Matthew 26:47–56)

Sometimes we're tempted to take a short cut in living out the will of God.

As Abraham and Sarah tried to hurry God's promise for an heir by using Hagar to bear a child, sometimes we too are carried away by our own impatience.

Sometimes we're tempted to accomplish God's will by our own devices.

As Rebecca helped her son Jacob to cheat his brother Esau, sometimes we too are carried away by our own desires.

Sometimes we're tempted to take matters into our own hands.

As Moses killed an Egyptian in anger over the oppression of his people, sometimes we too are carried away by our own anger.

But God's will cannot be accomplished by our own short cuts, manipulations, or anger.

It can only be accomplished as we follow that good and perfect and acceptable will that God sets before us.

Jesus showed us the way on the night of his arrest, for he chose God's will of the cross in spite of the agony of his own heart.

While he was still speaking, Judas came, one of the twelve, and with him a great crowd with swords and clubs, from the chief priests and the elders of the people. Now the betrayer had given them a sign, saying, "The one I shall kiss is the man; seize him." And he came up to Jesus at once and said, "Hail, Master!" And he kissed him. Jesus said to him, "Friend, why are you here?" Then they came up and laid hands on Jesus and seized him. (vv. 47–50)

Jesus chose God's will of the cross over the sword of self-defense.

And behold, one of those who were with Jesus stretched out his hand and drew his sword, and struck the slave of the high priest, and cut off his ear. Then Jesus said to him, "Put your sword back into its place; for all who take the sword will perish by the sword." (vv. 51, 52)

Jesus chose God's will of the cross over the way of supernatural intervention.

"Do you think that I cannot appeal to my Father, and he will at once send me more than twelve legions of angels? But how then should the scriptures be fulfilled, that it must be so?" (vv. 53, 54)

Jesus chose God's will of the cross over the temptation to flee from danger.

At that hour Jesus said to the crowds, "Have you come out as against a robber, with swords and clubs to capture me? Day after day I sat in the temple teaching, and you did not seize me. But all this has taken place, that the scriptures of the prophets might be fulfilled." Then all the disciples forsook him and fled. (vv. 55, 56)

Prayer: Dear God, sometimes your way may seem slow, painful, or unfair to us. But grant us courage to choose your will in spite of the obstacles we may face from our own hearts or the actions of others. Amen.

Delivered Up 46

Introduction: After Jesus' arrest, it seemed as if his opponents had finally gained the upper hand. But even then God remained sovereign over all.

Reading: (Matthew 26:59–66)

After his arrest in the garden of Gethsemane, Jesus was taken before a night session of the Jewish council, even though Jewish law required criminal cases to be heard only during the day.

Now the chief priests and the whole council sought false testimony against Jesus that they might put him to death, but they found none, though many false witnesses came forward. (vv. 59, 60a)

Finally, two witnesses were found who gave distorted accounts of Jesus' words concerning his bodily death and resurrection.

At last two came forward and said, "This fellow said, 'I am able to destroy the temple of God, and to build it in three days.' " (vv. 60b, 61)

This charge of blasphemy was untrue, but Jesus' opponents seized it as an excuse to try him.

And the high priest stood up and said, "Have you no answer to make? What is it that these men testify against you?" (v. 62)

When Jesus did not answer this false charge, the high priest came to the real reason for Jesus' arrest and trial.

But Jesus was silent. And the high priest said to him, "I adjure you by the living God, tell us if you are the Christ, the Son of God." (v. 63)

To this charge, Jesus replied with an assertion of divine authority as God's Chosen One.

Jesus said to him, "You have said so. But I tell you, hereafter you will see the Son of man seated at the right hand of Power, and coming on the clouds of heaven." (v. 64)

The high priest wasted no time in passing judgment on Jesus' claim to be the promised Messiah.

Then the high priest tore his robes, and said, "He has uttered blasphemy. Why do we still need witnesses? You have now heard his blasphemy. What is your judgment?" (vv. 65, 66a)

Although Jewish law required a guilty verdict to be delayed until the following day, the members of the Jewish council did not wait to pronounce sentence.

They answered, "He deserves death." (v. 66b)

The members of the council met unlawfully to condemn the author of all righteousness.

Yet Jesus himself chose to suffer the arrest, trial, and humiliation at their hands.

The members of the council sought false witness to condemn the author of all truth.

Yet Jesus himself chose to disclose his own identity.

The members of the council passed the death sentence unjustly to condemn the author of all justice.

Yet Jesus himself chose to lay down his own life.

Meditation/Discussion: What would you have done if you had been a member of this council? How do you address injustice when you see it today?

Sifted Like Wheat 47

Introduction: Our God, we thank you for your presence with us at all times. In failure and success, in depression and joy, in faithfulness and unfaithfulness, we know that you are there.

Reading: (Matthew 26:69–75)

On the night he was betrayed, Jesus told his disciple Peter that he would be sifted like wheat. Peter's faith would be tested, and he would deny Jesus three times.

But Peter and all the other disciples said they would stand with Jesus even if it meant their own deaths.

As it turned out, their words were far braver than their deeds. At Jesus' arrest, all of the disciples deserted him.

Even Peter, who followed Jesus and his captors as far as the courtyard of the high priest, could not bring himself to admit his identity as one of Jesus' disciples.

Now Peter was sitting outside in the courtyard. And a maid came up to him, and said, "You also were with Jesus the Galilean." But he denied it before them all, saying, "I do not know what you mean." (vv. 69, 70)

Sometimes we are like Peter, our God. We deny you before others when they confront us with the truth.

And when he went out to the porch, another maid saw him, and she said to the bystanders, "This man was with Jesus of Nazareth." And again he denied it with an oath, "I do not know the man." (vv. 71, 72)

Sometimes we are like Peter, our God. We deny you before others because we are afraid.

After a little while the bystanders came up and said to Peter, "Certainly you are also one of them, for your accent betrays you." Then he began to invoke a curse on himself and to swear, "I do not know the man." And immediately the cock crowed. (vv. 73, 74)

Sometimes we are like Peter, our God. We deny you before others and so betray both you and ourselves.

And Peter remembered the saying of Jesus, "Before the cock crows, you will deny me three times." And he went out and wept bitterly. (v. 75)

Sometimes we are like Peter, our God. We deny you before others and are dismayed at our own failure to be faithful.

We are sifted like wheat. The people and the situations we meet every day demand a response. In the way we relate to them we confess the strength or the weakness of our commitment to you.

We are weary for rest. We are tired of our own dishonesty with you, with others, and with ourselves. We are tired of our own fears and failures.

Like Peter, we long for restored relationship with you.

We turn to you for new courage and fresh commitment, glad for your acceptance and confident of your enabling power.

Like Peter, we receive with thanks your forgiveness for our failures and your grace to renew our walk with you. Amen.

Meditation/Discussion: Think of a time when you were untrue to God and to yourself as Peter was when he denied knowing Jesus. What will you do differently next time?

Let Christ Be Crucified 48

Introduction: When the days drew near for Jesus to be received up, he set his face to go to Jerusalem. (Luke 9:51)

Reading: (Matthew 27:15–18, 20–23)

Jesus deliberately set his course for Jerusalem and his own death, for he knew it was all part of God's plan.

He himself had predicted his arrest, trial, and crucifixion. And on the night of his arrest, he did not think to save himself, but to save the world through his own death.

After his arrest and trial before the Jewish council, Jesus stood on trial once more, this time before the Roman governor, Pontius Pilate.

Now at the feast the governor was accustomed to release for the crowd any one prisoner whom they wanted. And they had then a notorious prisoner, called Barabbas. (vv. 15, 16)

In Barabbas, Pilate saw an opportunity to avoid condemning Jesus, while at the same time keeping peace with the Jewish leaders, who wanted Jesus put to death.

So when they had gathered, Pilate said to them, "Whom do you want me to release for you, Barabbas or Jesus who is called Christ?" For he knew that it was out of envy that they had delivered him up. (vv. 17, 18)

Pilate was responsible for turning the decision over to the people.

Now the chief priests and the elders persuaded the people to ask for Barabbas and destroy Jesus. (v. 20)

The Jewish leaders were responsible for Jesus' arrest and for bringing him to trial before Pilate. Now they were also responsible for urging the people to ask for Jesus' death.

The governor again said to them, "Which of the two do you want me to release for you?" And they said, "Barabbas." (v. 21)

The people were responsible for following the false lead of the chief priests and elders. They were responsible for demanding Jesus' death.

Pilate said to them, "Then what shall I do with Jesus who is called Christ?" They all said, "Let him be crucified." And he said, "Why, what evil had he done?" But they shouted all the more, "Let him be crucified." (vv. 22, 23)

Like the Jewish leaders, who led their people to demand Jesus' death, sometimes we fail to fulfill our responsibilities to lead people in God's way.

Our God, teach us to exercise our responsibilities with care, that we may lead others in your truth.

Like Pilate, who gave in to the cries of the people, sometimes we set aside our responsibilities as if they are not ours under God.

Our God, teach us to accept our responsibilities without fear, that we may do your will.

Like the crowds, who turned against Jesus, sometimes we abandon our responsibilities that we owe to God.

Our God, teach us to carry out our responsibilities with commitment to you, that we may be faithful in all things. Amen.

Meditation/Discussion: What areas of responsibility has God given you as individuals or as a team? How can you assist each other in meeting them?

Man of Sorrows 49

Introduction: Then they spat in his face, and struck him; and some slapped him, saying, "Prophesy to us, you Christ! Who is it that struck you?" (Matthew 26:67, 68)

Reading: (Matthew 27:35–44)

Even after the injustice of Jesus' arrest and trial before both Jewish and Roman authorities, even after the insulting treatment before the Sanhedrin, even after the shouts of the crowd before Pilate, even after the scourging and other physical abuse at the hands of the soldiers, Jesus' agony was not yet over.

He suffered the burden of his own cross as he walked through the streets of Jerusalem to the place of execution.

He suffered the brutality of crucifixion and the indignity of the soldiers gambling for his clothes.

And when they had crucified him, they divided his garments among them by casting lots; then they sat down and kept watch over him there. (vv. 35, 36)

He suffered the injustice of being put to death as a lawbreaker, in the company of other lawbreakers.

And over his head they put the charge against him, which read, "This is Jesus the King of the Jews." Then two robbers were crucified with him, one on the right and one on the left. (vv. 37, 38)

He suffered the taunts of those who came to watch the crucifixions.

And those who passed by derided him, wagging their heads and saying, "You who would destroy the temple and build it in three days, save yourself! If you are the Son of God, come down from the cross." (vv. 39, 40)

He suffered further ridicule from the Jewish authorities.

So also the chief priests, with the scribes and elders, mocked him, saying, "He saved others; he cannot save himself. He is the King of Israel; let him come down now from the cross, and we will believe in him. He trusts in God; let God deliver him now, if he desires him; for he said, 'I am the Son of God.' " (vv. 41–43)

He suffered the contempt of his fellow victims who were crucified at his side.

And the robbers who were crucified with him also reviled him in the same way. (v. 44)

Jesus suffered the burden of the cross.

He is the man of sorrows, who stands with all those who carry the burdens of this world.

Jesus suffered the brutality of the cross.

He is the man of sorrows, who stands with all those who suffer the cruelties of this world.

Jesus suffered the indignity of the cross.

He is the man of sorrows, who stands with all those who bear the taunting blows of this world.

Jesus suffered the injustice of the cross.

He is the man of sorrows, who stands with all those who endure the abuse of this world, even as he himself endured to the end.

Prayer: Jesus is the man of sorrows, who stands with us all until God's peace and justice reign throughout the earth. Amen.

The Cross 50

Introduction: And being found in human form Jesus humbled himself and became obedient unto death, even death on a cross. (Philippians 2:8)

Reading: (Matthew 27:45-54)

Jesus was no stranger to the suffering of this world.

He grew up as a Jew in a country occupied by Roman forces.

He was misunderstood by the people of his home town and even by members of his own family.

He was repeatedly questioned by the religious authorities who sought to destroy him.

He was betrayed by a close companion and deserted by a number of other friends.

He was arrested unjustly and endured both verbal and physical abuse.

And once the authorities succeeded in convicting him of blasphemy, he was put to death on the cross.

Now from the sixth hour there was darkness over all the land until the ninth hour. And about the ninth hour Jesus cried with a loud voice, "Eli, Eli, lama sabach-thani?" that is, "My God, my God, why hast thou forsaken me?" (vv. 45, 46)

As Jesus alone on the cross suffered the sins of the world, he cried out as if God had finally forsaken him.

And some of the bystanders hearing it said, "This man is calling Elijah." (v. 47)

But Jesus had not despaired of God's presence. His cry was a prayer to God.

And one of them at once ran and took a sponge, filled it with vinegar, and put it on a reed, and gave it to him to drink. (v. 48)

But Jesus had not asked for someone or something to deaden his pain. His cry was a longing for God.

But the others said, "Wait, let us see whether Elijah will come to save him." (v. 49)

But Jesus had not called on Elijah to save him. In fact, his next cry was a commitment of his spirit to God.

And Jesus cried again with a loud voice and yielded up his spirit. (v. 50)

By his suffering and death, Jesus opened the way to a new freedom to approach God and a new freedom from the power of death.

And behold, the curtain of the temple was torn in two, from top to bottom; and the earth shook, and the rocks were split; the tombs also were opened, and many bodies of the saints who had fallen asleep were raised, and coming out of the tombs after his resurrection they went into the holy city and appeared to many. (vv. 51–53)

By his suffering and death, Jesus brought a new understanding of the power of God.

When the centurion and those who were with him, keeping watch over Jesus, saw the earthquake and what took place, they were filled with awe, and said, "Truly this was the Son of God!" (v. 54)

Prayer: Our Savior Jesus, we thank you for your life, suffering, death, and resurrection. May we follow your example of commitment to God in the circumstances of our own lives. Amen.

Good News 51

Introduction: Praise God for the good news we've received in the person of the risen Christ. Amen.

Reading: (Matthew 28:1–10)

God is a giver of good news.

When God chose Mary to bring Jesus into the world, God sent an angel to tell her of the Spirit's work.

At Jesus' birth, God sent an angel with a whole company of angels to announce good will to all the earth.

Now after Jesus' death, God sent yet another angel with a new message.

Now after the sabbath, toward the dawn of the first day of the week, Mary Magdalene and the other Mary went to see the sepulcher. (v. 1)

They had been present at Jesus' death and burial, and now at the tomb, God sent an angel to greet them.

And behold, there was a great earthquake; for an angel of the Lord descended from heaven and came and rolled back the stone, and sat upon it. His appearance was like lightning, and his raiment white as snow. And for fear of him the guards trembled and became like dead men. (vv. 2–4)

The guards were overcome with fear and were unable to receive God's message.

But the angel said to the women, "Do not be afraid; for I know that you seek Jesus who was crucified. He is not here; for he has risen, as he said. Come, see the place where he lay. Then go quickly and tell his disciples that he has risen from the dead, and behold, he is going before you to Galilee; there you will see him. Lo, I have told you." (vv. 5–7)

Jesus' resurrection was good news of great joy, and the women were eager to spread the word.

So they departed quickly from the tomb with fear and great joy, and ran to tell his disciples. (v. 8)

Jesus' resurrection was good news to celebrate in worship, and the women praised the risen Christ.

And behold, Jesus met them and said, "Hail!" And they came up and took hold of his feet and worshiped him. (v. 9)

Jesus' resurrection was good news meant to be shared, and the women took the message to the other disciples.

Then Jesus said to them, "Do not be afraid; go and tell my brethren to go to Galilee, and there they will see me." (v. 10)

As God gave good news to Mary Magdalene and to the other Mary, so God also gives good news to us. Christ is the living God!

Therefore let us rejoice!

We will rejoice with great joy!

Let us worship the risen Christ, our God.

We will worship God in spirit and in truth.

Let us proclaim the good news.

We will proclaim the risen Christ in word and deed.

Prayer: Our gracious God, like the women at the tomb may we receive your good news with joy, respond with true worship, and proclaim it gladly to those around us. Amen.

God With Us Still 52

Introduction: Our God is a living God, who is present with us here, who calls us by name, who works in us and through us for God's glory and our good. Praise be to God.

Reading: (Matthew 28:16–20)

When Jesus appeared to Mary Magdalene and the other Mary after his resurrection, he sent them to tell the other disciples to meet him in Galilee.

Now the eleven disciples went to Galilee, to the mountain to which Jesus had directed them. (v. 16)

They came with a mixture of joy and fear, with a measure of both faith and disbelief.

And when they saw him they worshiped him; but some doubted. (v. 17)

But to all of them, Jesus proclaimed his power as the resurrected Christ.

And Jesus came and said to them, "All authority in heaven and on earth has been given to me." (v. 18)

On the basis of this authority, Jesus sent his disciples out on a great mission and promised his own presence with them.

"Go therefore and make disciples of all the nations, baptizing them in the name of the Father and of the Son and of the Holy Spirit, teaching them to observe all that I have commanded you; and lo, I am with you always, to the close of the age." (vv. 19, 20)

Jesus' work did not end with his crucifixion, death, and burial.

He rose again as he promised and appeared to many.

Jesus' work did not end with his resurrection and ascension.

He met his disciples in Galilee and gave them a great commission.

Jesus' work did not end with the first disciples of his earthly life.

He continues to call men and women into relationship with God and to send them out with that same proclamation.

As Jesus met with his first disciples in Galilee after his resurrection, so God meets with us today in our own time and place.

Thank you, God, for the communion we share with you. May we honestly worship you with all our heart, mind, and soul.

As Jesus sent his disciples out to make other disciples among all the nations, so God sends us out today to our own world.

Thank you, God, for entrusting us with the task of continuing Jesus' own work. May we faithfully proclaim your teaching in all we say and do.

As Jesus promised his presence to his disciples, so God promises to be with us today and even to the end of the age.

Thank you, God, for the assurance of your own presence with us. May we continually abide in your love and know the fullness of your joy. Amen.

Prayer: Our God of heaven and earth, we thank you for Jesus Christ, the same yesterday, today, and forever. May we accept the commission to proclaim your reign, knowing that Jesus is still our Immanuel, God with us. Amen.

This is the Lord's doing;
it is marvelous in our eyes.
This is the day which the Lord has made;
let us rejoice and be glad in it.
Psalm 118:23, 24

Thanksgiving

Introduction: On this special day of thanksgiving, we ask for a true spirit of thanks to carry with us throughout the year.

Reading: (Matthew 14:14–21)

Come, let us enter the gates of our God with thanksgiving.

We give thanks to God the Creator, our Maker, who made all things visible and invisible.

Come, let us fill God's courts with praise.

We give thanks to God the Spirit, our Sustainer, who upholds the universe with a breath.

Come, let us give thanks to God and bless the name of the Holy One.

We give thanks to God the Eternal Word, our Savior, who became flesh for our sake.

Now when Jesus first heard about the death of John the Baptist, he went by boat to a lonely place, but many people followed him there.

As he went ashore he saw a great throng; and he had compassion on them, and healed their sick. (v. 14)

We give thanks for God's healing power, which brings wholeness to human life.

When it was evening, the disciples came to him and said, "This is a lonely place, and the day is now over; send the crowds away to go into the villages and buy food for themselves." Jesus said, "They need not go away; you give them something to eat." (vv. 15, 16)

We give thanks for God's heart of compassion, which longs to give rest to the weary and food to the hungry.

They said to him, "We have only five loaves here and two fish." And he said, "Bring them here to me." Then he ordered the crowds to sit down on the grass; and taking the five loaves and the two fish he looked up to heaven, and blessed, and broke and gave the loaves to the disciples, and the disciples gave them to the crowds. (vv. 17–19)

We give thanks for God's enabling work, which empowers and equips God's people for service.

And they all ate and were satisfied. And they took up twelve baskets full of the broken pieces left over. And those who ate were about five thousand men, besides women and children. (vv. 20, 21)

We give thanks for God's provision, which satisfies us so fully with good things.

We give thanks to God the Eternal Word, our Redeemer, who lived and worked on this earth.

We give thanks to God and bless the Holy One.

We give thanks to God the Spirit, our Guide, who teaches us all things.

We enter the gates of our God with thanksgiving and fill God's courts with praise.

We give thanks to God the Creator, our Sovereign, who reigns over all and for all time. Amen.

Meditation/Discussion: Which statement of thankfulness in the responsive reading do you identify with the most closely?

Prayer: Our God, we are thankful for all that you have been to us and all that you have done for us in the last year. May we continue to be thankful people, always conscious of your presence and provision for us. Amen.

Christmas

Introduction: We take this time together to reflect on the meaning of Christ's birth. May we learn to appreciate Christmas in a new and deeper way this season. Amen.

Reading: (Matthew 2:1–12)

Now when Jesus was born in Bethlehem of Judea in the days of Herod the king, behold, wise men from the East came to Jerusalem, saying, "Where is he who has been born king of the Jews? For we have seen his star in the East, and have come to worship him." (vv. 1, 2)

The wise men responded to the sign of Jesus' birth with a personal journey to worship the Christ child. But not everyone who heard about the new king responded in such a positive way.

When Herod the king heard this, he was troubled, and all Jerusalem with him; (v. 3)

Herod was troubled with this talk of a new king, for he already held the title of king of the Jews. And the people of Jerusalem were troubled, for they were afraid of what Herod might do in his anger.

And assembling all the chief priests and scribes of the people, he inquired of them where the Christ was to be born. (v. 4)

From the prophet Micah, the priests and the scribes were able to tell Herod what he wanted to know.

They told him, "In Bethlehem of Judea; for so it is written by the prophet: 'And you, O Bethlehem, in the land of Judah, are by no means least among the rulers of Judah; for from you shall come a ruler who will govern my people Israel.' " (vv. 5, 6)

But Herod was not content with their report. He needed more detailed information if he would destroy this potential rival.

Then Herod summoned the wise men secretly and ascertained from them what time the star appeared; and he sent them to Bethlehem, saying, "Go and search diligently for the child, and when you have found him bring me word, that I too may come and worship him." (vv. 7, 8)

So the wise men continued their search for the young king, and God directed their path.

When they had heard the king they went their way; and lo, the star which they had seen in the East went before them, till it came to rest over the place where the child was. (v. 9)

When the wise men were finally ushered into the presence of the Christ child, they celebrated the occasion with great joy, sincere worship, and the offering of gifts.

When they saw the star, they rejoiced exceedingly with great joy; and going into the house they saw the child with Mary his mother, and they fell down and worshiped him. Then, opening their treasures, they offered him gifts, gold and frankincense and myrrh. (vv. 10, 11)

When it was time for the wise men to return to their own homes, God again directed their path.

And being warned in a dream not to return to Herod, they departed to their own country by another way. (v. 12)

Meditation/Discussion: In what ways has God led your own spiritual pilgrimage?

Prayer: Our God, we thank you for the guidance given to us through your Spirit. May we respond to you as the wise men did, with great joy, sincere worship, and the offering of ourselves. Amen.

Easter

Introduction: Our God, we thank you for this Easter season. Lead us now as we reflect together on the meaning of Jesus' death and resurrection. Amen.

Reading: (Matthew 16:21–28)

From that time Jesus began to show his disciples that he must go to Jerusalem and suffer many things from the elders and chief priests and scribes, and be killed, and on the third day be raised. (v. 21)

But Peter didn't understand how these events could take place in the life of Jesus, who exercised authority over demons, who stilled the waters, and who multiplied the loaves and fishes to feed a crowd of people.

And Peter took him and began to rebuke him, saying, "God forbid, Lord! This shall never happen to you." (v. 22)

Yet Jesus knew God's plan for human history could not be fulfilled without his own death.

But he turned and said to Peter, "Get behind me, Satan! You are a hindrance to me; for you are not on the side of God, but of men." (v. 23)

In fact, Jesus' way of suffering servanthood and resurrection to newness of life is the way for all of his followers.

Then Jesus told his disciples, "If any man would come after me, let him deny himself and take up his cross and follow me. For whoever would save his life will lose it, and whoever loses his life for my sake will find it." (vv. 24, 25)

The life that God gives is more precious than all the world.

"For what will it profit a man, if he gains the whole world and forfeits his life? Or what shall a man give in return for his life?" (v. 26)

But while Jesus spoke of his suffering and death, he also foretold his resurrection and glorification.

"For the Son of man is to come with his angels in the glory of his Father, and then he will repay every man for what he has done. Truly, I say to you, there are some standing here who will not taste death before they see the Son of man coming in his kingdom." (vv. 27, 28)

So if we want to follow Jesus, we must also lose our lives.

We die to our own ambitions and to our own desires, so that we might follow the way of God.

If we want to follow Jesus, we must also take up the cross.

We die to our own ways of doing things and to our own standards of success, so that we might follow the way of God.

We die to this world.

And we are raised to new life.

We die to self.

And we live to God.

Meditation/Discussion: What newness of life have you experienced in following Jesus? What obstacles have you encountered?

Prayer: Almighty God, who raised Jesus from the dead, we ask you also to raise us up to a new purpose and a new strength to follow you. Amen.

Let the word of Christ dwell in you richly, teach and admonish one another in all wisdom, and sing psalms and hymns and spiritual songs with thankfulness in your hearts to God.
And whatever you do, in word or deed, do everything in the name of the Lord Jesus, giving thanks to God the Father through him.

Colossians 3:16, 17

Take Time for Meditation and Discussion

Background to the Gospel of Matthew

Author: Not identified from the text of the gospel. Yet from the language and content of the book, we know the author to be a Jewish Christian. Tradition identifies him as one of Jesus' twelve apostles, the former tax gatherer known as Matthew or Levi.

Audience: Written for a primarily Jewish audience familiar with the Old Testament, which is often quoted in the gospel. Yet the book's appeal is not limited to Jewish readers, for it has proven to be the most widely read of the four gospels.

Aim: Bears witness to the events of Jesus' life, death, and resurrection, with an emphasis on Jesus' teaching.

Meditation/Discussion Questions

If you need some additional guidance for your meditation and discussion together, you may want to consider one of the following:

1. What is the main point of the responsive reading? Do you agree with it? Why or why not?
2. Which key word or sentence best summarizes the point of the responsive reading? Is there any specific event in your life which illustrates the same point?
3. Which verse of the Scripture passage best summarizes the point of the responsive reading? What other Scripture passages does it bring to mind?
4. If you were to give this responsive reading a new title, what would it be? Why?

5. Who are the main characters in the Scripture passage? What emotions do they display and why? To what extent do you identify with them?
6. Did you learn anything new about God or about yourself from the responsive reading? How will your thinking and/or behavior change?
7. What questions does the responsive reading leave unanswered for you? Discuss them with your partner. You may also want to make a note of these for further research.
8. Your own topic.

Take Time for Prayer

If you are new to the practice of joint devotions, you may feel a little awkward sharing and praying together at first. To get yourselves started, just glance through the *Sharing Together* list below, and try the one or two suggestions that best suit your needs and personalities. Then continue your conversation in prayer with one of the suggestions from the *Praying Together* list which follows. As you continue to meet together, you will probably want to use different combinations of the items listed or add others of your own.

Sharing Together

1. What is the best thing that happened to you today (or this week)? Does it affect any other person either positively or negatively?
2. What is the worst thing that happened to you today (or this week)? Is there anything good about it? What would you do differently next time? What would you do the same?
3. What is the one thing you spent most of your time thinking about today (or this week)? How is it a cause for praise and/or concern?
4. What is the one thing you look forward to the most today (or this week)?
5. What is your greatest responsibility or task today (or this week)? What personal qualities or other resources do you need to meet this challenge?
6. What decisions do you need to make today (or this week)? How can your partner encourage you and/or help you clarify your thinking?
7. What joys do you experience in your partnership together? For what qualities in your partner are you particularly thankful?

8. What obstacle do you see to the continuing growth of your partnership? What steps do you need to take to resolve it? You may find it easier to follow through with some concrete action if you write these down first.
9. How can the two of you become more effective as a team in ministering to your family, friends, and the world around you? You may want to write down your goals and review them periodically.

Praying Together

1. Pray together silently about the things you have discussed. You may want to use the short sentence completion prayers in suggestion 4. One of you could close your prayer time with a simple "amen" or with reading aloud the closing prayer where provided in the devotional.
2. Have one person mention a topic for prayer and then pray about it silently until that person introduces a new topic. Alternate the responsibility of suggesting topics if you wish.
3. Have one person read aloud a prayer. Try the closing prayer where provided in the devotional reading, or one of the prayers from the Bible such as Matthew 6:9b–13 (the Lord's prayer) or Psalms 8, 46, 67, or 113.
4. Pray aloud with short sentence completion prayers:
   "Our Creator God, thank you for ______________."
   "O Living Word, strengthen us to ______________."
   "Holy Spirit, guide us in ______________."
5. Pray aloud spontaneously in your own words about the things you have discussed.